BUILDING YOUR
HIGH SCHOOL
FOOTBALL
PROGRAM

In Pursuit of Excellence

JOSEPH G. PACELLI

Leisure Press
Champaign, Illinois

Library of Congress Cataloging-in-Publication Data

Pacelli, Joseph G., 1934–
   Building your high school football program.

   Bibliography: p.
   1. Football—Coaching. I. Title.
GV956.6.P32   1987   796.332'07'7   86-27706
ISBN 0-88011-286-7

Developmental Editor: Steve Houseworth
Copy Editor: Lise Rodgers
Assistant Editor: Janet Beals
Production Director: Ernie Noa
Assistant Production Director: Lezli Harris
Typesetter: Sonnie Bowman
Text Design: Keith Blomberg
Text Layout: Denise Mueller
Cover Design: Jack Davis
Printed By: Braun-Brumfield, Inc.

ISBN: 0-88011-286-7

Printed in the United States of America

10 9 8 7 6 5 4 3 2 1

Leisure Press
A division of Human Kinetics Publishers, Inc.
Box 5076, Champaign, IL 61820
1-800-DIAL-HKP
1-800-334-3665 (in Illinois)

Dedication

To Larry
Thanks for the inspiration
and
To Alesta
For the help and patience

Acknowledgments

The author would like to acknowledge with gratitude and appreciation, the following persons who, either through personal interview or clinic lecture, have contributed to the ideas expressed in this text.

Joe Paterno, Head Coach, Pennsylvania State University.
Lou Holtz, Head Coach, Notre Dame University, IN.
Jack Elway, Head Coach, Stanford University, CA.
Robert Shoup, Head Coach, California Lutheran University.
Bo Schembechler, Head Coach, University of Michigan.
Grant Teaff, Head Coach, Baylor University, TX.
Patrick Hill, Daniel Webster College, NH.
John Reardon, Head Coach, Rio Mesa High School, CA.
Nick Hyder, Head Coach, Valdosta High School, GA.
Phil Zukowski, Head Coach, Adna High School, WA.
Bob McQueen, Head Coach, Temple High School, TX.
Jim Carberry, Former Head Coach, Boise High School, ID.
Ty Cotton, Head Coach, Cascade High School, MT.
Max Hawk, Head Coach, Yankton High School, SD.
Joe Hoskins, Head Coach, Henry Ford High School, MI.
Bron Bacevich, Head Coach, Roger Bacon (Cincinnati) High School, OH.
Paul Nestor, Head Coach, Bishop Ready High School, OH.
Gordon Wood, Head Coach, Brownwood High School, TX.
Larry Edwards, Head Coach, Calabasas High School, CA.
Gene Zeller, Head Coach, Whittier High School, CA.
Frank Greminger, Head Coach, Agoura High School, CA.
Jim Emerling, Head Coach, West Valley, Canoga Park, CA.
Edward W. Sutton, MD, Valley Medical Group, Fresno, CA.

Sonny P. Cobble, MD, Orthopaedic Surgeon, Los Angeles, CA.

Phillip H. McFarland, MD, Orthopaedic Surgeon, Los Angeles, CA.

Hedda Bolgar, PhD, Clinical Psychologist, Los Angeles, CA.

Gary Tuthill, DC, Tuthill Athletic Rehabilitation Institute, CA.

John Thie, DC, Thie Chiropractic Clinic, Pasadena, CA.

William Hunt, RPT, Medical Center Physical Therapy, Malibu, CA.

David Crawley, ATC, Certified Athletic Trainer, Northridge, CA.

George Allen, Former Pro-Football Head Coach, Palos Verdes, CA.

Phil Hoover, Former College Freshman Head Coach, Reseda, CA.

Michael Shepherd, Former High School Head Coach, Malibu, CA.

Steve Bennett, Former High School Head Coach, Ojai, CA.

Darryl Smith, Former Youth Football Head Coach, Calabasas, CA.

Cary Lipman, Former Youth Football Head Coach, Plainfield, NJ.

Bob Perez, Team Action Sporting Goods, Costa Mesa, CA.

And a special thank you to Head Coach Tom Landry and the staff of the Dallas Cowboys Football Organization.

The author would further like to acknowledge the many coaches, administrators, physicians, technicians, trainers, and nutritionists who have published interesting and informative articles in the following journals:

Scholastic Coach
50 West 44th Street
New York, NY 10036

Athletic Journal
1719 Howard Street
Evanston, IL 60202

Several of these articles contained valuable information that was extremely useful in formulating the presentation of this book.

Contents

Foreword

My last year in the pros was spent with the legendary Coach Vince Lombardi and his 1961 NFL Champion Green Bay Packers. That year I also started my last year in medical school, and thus some of the minor doctoring in the training room fell to me. On Friday afternoons at the behest of Paul Hornung (and because we kept winning after the practice was instituted), I gave 25 to 30 B-12 shots. It was on one of these days that Coach Lombardi came into the training room to see what all the commotion was about. Seizing an opportunity to be a little serious and a lot funny, I said, "Coach, I think I should be getting two salaries—one for being with the team and one for doctoring." Without a moment's hesitation he looked up at me with a twinkle in his eye and said, "Son, you're just damn lucky to be here!"

And so I was, as will be those of you who are lucky enough to use and study Coach Joe Pacelli's *Building Your High School Football Program: In Pursuit of Excellence.* As Coach Pacelli himself says, "Luck happens when preparation meets opportunity." From this book, you will learn how to prepare for the opportunities ahead. All of us learn by experience—a lot of it bitter. But with the help of an experienced student of the game like Coach Pacelli, maybe some of that bitterness can be avoided.

OK, you might ask, so what does Ed Sutton know about coaching high school football? I'll admit not much in the technical sense, but I have certainly played for enough coaches to know a good coach when I see one. In the year that I played at Sylva, North Carolina under Joe Hunt, we won the first of his many high school championships. I just assumed it must be easy to coach, because Coach Hunt did it with such apparent ease. I found out differently between my first team and my last team, both champions. During that time, I played for some good teams, and for some bad teams. I played for great coaches, and for a few coaches who were disorganized and did not know how to handle men or get the most from their talents. Someone once said that Coach Lombardi knew when to pat us on the head or kick us in the butt. Many of us thought he got it mixed up a lot. However he used his ploys, they obviously worked for him. My late, great friend, defensive tackle Henry Jordan, once said, ''Coach Lombardi treated us all alike, just like dogs.'' He didn't mean that, but you have to appreciate what his remark reveals: the love-hate relationship and ambivalent feelings that exist between a coach and his players, even in the best of circumstances.

Looking back, I now believe that many of the poorer coaches I have known could have benefited a great deal from some of the insight, organization, and procedural information in this book. The winners—including my college coach Jim Tatum at the University of North Carolina and Coach Jim Lee Howell of the New York Giants—have always been organized and have known the secret of delegating authority to extremely competent assistant coaches. The story has it that once, before a critical Giants game, a reporter found Jim Lee Howell with his feet up on the desk casually reading a paper. When the reporter asked Howell why he wasn't hard at work preparing for the next day's game, Howell replied that he was: If the reporter didn't believe him, he could check the next two rooms. On doing so, the reporter found Howell's assistants—Tom Landry in one room and Vince Lombardi in the other—both burning the midnight oil. Now that's organization!

But, you may ask, what does this guy Joe Pacelli know about football or how to coach it? Well, I have known Coach Pacelli for many years. I know his background as a player, as a successful businessman, and as a football coach. I know that this book will be valuable to the reader because the author is intelligent, thorough, organized, insightful, and has a deep understanding of football at every level. I know that this book has been a labor of love for Joe. My advice to the reader is to use it as if it were a guidebook or a cookbook: Add your own spice to it; add lessons from your own repertoire. At the very least, this book will help soften the rough spots for you—of that I am sure. Coach Joe Pacelli, a coach's coach, has analyzed and chronicled for you—the next generation of coaches—one more tool to use in your pursuit of excellence.

But how do I know, personally, that he is such a great coach and teacher? Over the years Joe Pacelli and I have watched many football games together. I have listened to his analysis, and discussed with him in great detail the action of these games. Not once, to my recollection, has he ever disagreed with me.

Edward W. Sutton, M.D.
Physician/Surgeon
NFL Alumnus

Preface

"Pursuit of Excellence" is neither a new nor an unusual precept. As a general principle, it has existed since the beginning of recorded history in almost every field of human endeavor. The ancient Egyptian architects, Greek philosophers, Roman legions, astronomers and explorers throughout the centuries, and Olympic athletes from ancient Greece to the present, have all focused upon the "Pursuit of Excellence." The ancient Greek philosopher Plato believed that excellence is infinite and can never truly be attained, only pursued—that ordinary people become extraordinary only by pursuing excellence. More recent thinking considers excellence a purely subjective goal to be judged on a relative basis; excellence is simply being "as good as you can be." However, from ancient to modern times, all philosophers agree that the "pursuit of excellence" is one of the most venerable efforts of mankind.

The purpose of this book is to apply this time-honored precept to the building of a high school football program; it is to examine in depth a subject that until this time has been treated only marginally, and only on occasion, by clinic lecturers or in periodicals. More than 12 years of coaching experience and 2 1/2 years of research have gone into the preparation of this book—the first of its kind, to the best of my knowledge, that is specifically and comprehensively devoted to the subject of building a high school football program. Nevertheless, much of what is contained within these pages is not original thinking. Many great coaches, administrators and psychologists have contributed concepts and philosophies that have been a strong influence in the development of this text. The book combines some previously espoused doctrines (which are consistent with my own thinking) and my personal philosophy into one, thorough adviser. It can clarify the complexities of preparation, organization, motivation, and discipline; and it can help take you from hoping you could win, to believing you should win.

Building Your High School Football Program: In Pursuit of Excellence is, as well, a comprehensive guide for both the young and for the more experienced coach ready to make an upward career move. The step from varsity assistant coach (or lower division head coach) to varsity head coach is a gigantic one—even within the same program. If a coach steps into an entirely new situation functioning as varsity head coach and, at the same time, bearing responsibility for building a consistently successful football program—the pressures can be enormous. If the coach is not properly prepared, he will almost certainly fail. These chapters are a detailed, step-by-step scenario designed to direct a coach in a sound method of preparation—a method specifically designed to obviate pitfalls and to pursue excellence in the building of a vital, winning high school football program.

This book was conceived with the purpose of equipping the serious-minded coach with a single source containing what is necessary to succeed as a high school head coach. Most high school football programs are not blessed with an abundance of football talent on a yearly basis. If you find this to be true in your situation, and you are searching for ways to produce a superior team, this book will help you to improve your program. A solid, consistent program is your best assurance of success.

Football is very simple in its basic principles, and I assume that most coaches ready to make a move to varsity head coach are thoroughly familiar with the Xs and Os of the game. If not (for I realize this may be a dangerous assumption to make), reams of valuable information stock library shelves throughout the country on the many ways to play the game. This book will concentrate on everything—except offense, defense, and special teams.

In attempting to be as concise as possible while including all the elements necessary for a complete and successful program, I have chosen to use an itemized format in many instances. Due, therefore, to the extensive number of lists, outlines, schedules, and charts in this book, I would suggest that the reader not try to commit such information to memory. Rather, after an initial reading, you will probably find it much more beneficial to refer to specific chapters as the need arises. This book deals with a rather broad spectrum of ideas within a large and complex subject. It is intended to be as much a reference source as it is a text.

Joseph G. Pacelli

Chapter 1

Preparing for Leadership

Exactly what is leadership? The dictionary defines it as "guiding, directing, moving others in a certain direction." It is, in fact, an ultimate form of giving, a total personal commitment to helping others. Leadership is an art form that can be achieved only through study, organization, planning and positive attitude training. Before we can influence the factors that control others' lives, we must be in control of those same factors in our own lives. A leader must be a doer, not a posturer—one who is able to view adversity as a challenge, and welcome the opportunity to take command in the face of it. A leader must have deep insight into character and have the ability to read it quickly. A good leader is decisive, but also democratic, involving subordinates in decisions and delegating responsibilities. Nothing is more damaging to the credibility of a leader than a dictatorial approach to subordinates. Such an approach destroys morale and kills incentive. On the other hand, a leader cannot seek group approval before making a decision. A leader's conduct should indicate a willingness to listen, but also a firm intent to make the final decisions.

Some people innately have many of these qualities; many more do not. Some people have a natural charm or charisma that gives them an edge in leadership. However, contrary to popular belief, leaders are not born. Leaders are made, and they are made by effort and hard work. In this chapter we will deal with the following steps to leadership:

Step 1: Self-Evaluation
Step 2: Positive Attitude Development
Step 3: Proper Use of Time
Step 4: Goal Planning
Step 5: Organization
Step 6: Motivation and Discipline
Step 7: Accepting Challenge

These are the seven steps to success in leadership.

Step 1: Self-Evaluation

People most frequently see only the "mirror image" of themselves. This is the image that we most often wish others to see. It is a human failing to perceive only our strengths and assets and none of our weaknesses and liabilities. Sometimes, though, we find it difficult to acknowledge our own shortcomings. This self-delusion and failure to perceive reality will most certainly work to our own detriment, and may even overshadow excellent job skills and performances. If you wish to take stock of yourself, make this step a valuable self-appraisal. Do not delude yourself that you already have all the answers and can learn nothing new of lasting benefit. This step is a relatively simple one that may be used to begin a more intense self-examination, or self-appraisal, process on a regular basis. Two types of inquiries are required for a proper self-evaluation. The first deals with personal character traits, and the second evaluates present management skills.

Begin your self-evaluation by using the following ideas to develop a series of questions on personal character. These questions should be designed to provoke serious self-appraisal; the more probing they are, the better.

This will probably be the most difficult part of the process, because you may tend to answer the questions as you write them. Make a special effort to resist this impulse by concentrating on asking the most probing questions possible. I suggest that you prepare all of the questions on all of these topics before you begin to write any answers. Develop the questions as if you were preparing an in-depth analysis for someone other than yourself, and don't hesitate to ask strongly pointed questions—after all, you will be the only one to see the answers.

Allow room after each question for a complete answer, and answer each question honestly. Unless you are extremely honest and thorough in developing both your questions and your answers, the effort will be fruitless. On the other hand, true and complete answers to in-depth questions will open the way to self-improvement, which is our aim.

The most important insight any leader can have is an understanding of one's own propensity for honesty. Ask yourself how honest you are, with yourself and with others. Your ability to achieve true success as a head coach (or as anything else, for that matter) hinges upon your personal integrity. To maintain your integrity, you must never compromise the truth. On the other hand, do not use honesty as an excuse for being cruel. Even though it is often necessary to be brutally honest with yourself, sometimes good sense and compassion dictate that honesty toward others be tempered with understanding. However, regardless of how tactful you can be, you must understand whether or not you now possess the courage and integrity to confront issues such as morality, fairness, prejudice, jeopardy, and responsibility with honesty.

The second personal characteristic to analyze is your capacity for trust. All leaders require the judgment to know who, what, when, and why to trust. Begin by asking yourself if you inspire trust in others and whether or not you have the ability to evaluate trustworthiness in someone else. It is imperative, after all, that a head coach delegate responsibility and authority to members of his staff and even to his players. The aim of your questions on this topic should be to discover the extent of your ability to read character. The key to building a successful football program, or even a business, lies in the ability of a leader to judge people and situations, to decide in whom he or she can place trust. Discover your own abilities and limitations in this area so that you can work to optimize them. Once you have developed this skill and can use it in your work, you will find that it allows an atmosphere of enthusiasm to develop within the program;

it encourages creativity, it stimulates motivation, and most of all, it solidifies team spirit.

Next, it is important to know the type of role model you are. Your credibility as a head coach depends more on how you conduct yourself than simply on the things that you say. The school administrators, the faculty, your staff, and especially your players, will all evaluate your behavior. They will quickly know if you are the kind of person who practices what you preach, or if you merely pay lip service to idealism; they will respond to you, or not, based upon this evaluation. With that in mind, you can see how important it is for you to understand these things about yourself before you attempt to lead others. Perhaps the most salient point to analyze here is whether or not you are or have been a good subordinate. Have you always given your best effort when working for others? If so, then you will be asking others to do only what you already do. You can then teach character not merely by telling, but by example. On the other hand, if you have not been a good subordinate, you will probably have a great deal of work to do on this part of your character before you can become a good role model.

Directly related to being a good role model is positive attitude. Think about your attitudes toward life and toward your chosen occupation of coaching. Ask yourself if you are generally a positive or a negative person, and, regardless of your coaching style, determine if your attitude on the field is positive or negative. The best way to decide this is to watch yourself at work: See if you tend to reinforce positive action; note whether or not you enhance an athlete's self-image; examine your own reactions to both winning and losing. A head coach with a positive attitude will have little trouble creating a successful program, and will likely receive considerable help from others both inside and outside the program.

The next personal characteristic you will need to evaluate is your motivation for wanting to be a high school football coach. Examine these motives closely. Most coaches claim the purest of intents: love of the game, delight in working with young people, and the opportunity to teach important values. These are truly the ideal reasons for wanting to be a football coach at this level, but all too often high school coaches are not drawn to this occupation by unadulterated idealism. Many times unrealistic expectations of power, glory, and adulation, or distorted concepts far more perverse, are the underlying stimuli that produce high school coaches. It is important that you clearly understand your own motives so that you can filter out impurities and bring any distortions into proper focus. It is common for people to desire recognition for their efforts, and reasonable to seek a certain degree of control in one's chosen field. However, one must always maintain the emotional judgment to keep these elements in perspective. The pursuit of excellence as a high school football coach requires hard work and a great deal of preparation. You cannot allow unrealistic, distorted thinking to dissuade you from this venerable goal.

The next thing you need to question is the amount of effort you have put into learning all aspects of the game. You must ask yourself whether or not you possess sufficient football expertise to be a head coach and if you have the ability to express yourself, both orally and in writing, so that you can communicate this knowledge to others. Also, consider if you have something of special value to offer a program. Determine just what your strengths and assets are, and how these things can help you to build a successful program. Then, honestly assess your liabilities and weaknesses. Think about what you are prepared to do to improve the quality of what you have to offer.

Once you have completed your questions and answers dealing with personal character traits, set them aside for a few days. In the meantime, begin to evaluate your management skills. While answering the following questions, try to use a comparative approach—that is, compare your abilities to the abilities of someone, in any occupation, who is excellent, from your point of view, in that specific area of administration:

- How do you manage your time? Do you waste time? Do you duplicate effort? What value do you put on your time?
- Are you an effective goal planner? How do you approach goal planning? Are your goals idealistic or realistic? What is your ultimate personal goal?
- Do you consider yourself to be an organized person? Do you consider good organization essential to success? Is your ability to organize developed enough to be a successful administrator?
- Do you feel that you are a good motivator? Do you believe in yourself and your ideas? Are you enthusiastic about those

things that you believe? How do you rate your ability to transmit your enthusiasm to others?

- Do you understand the tenets of proper discipline? Are you a disciplined person? Have you ever used discipline effectively?
- Do you ever challenge yourself above the norm? Do you enjoy a challenge? How do you challenge yourself? How do you respond to a crisis situation? How do you react to pressure?

These management skill topics will be developed in depth in Steps 3 through 7 of this chapter. It might be helpful for you to complete a draft of the preceding question-and-answer exercise before reading the rest of this chapter. Then, when you have finished chapter 1, return to your questions and answers with a fresh, more insightful view. Underline the answers that indicate strengths or assets with a blue pen, and the answers that indicate weaknesses or liabilities with a red pen. You will then be able to evaluate yourself more effectively, and immediately begin developing a program for self-improvement.

Step 2: Positive Attitude Development

In 1962, several years after graduating from college, a crisis occurred in my life—a life that, until that time, was relatively mundane and unfulfilling, without direction or real purpose. That crisis, and more directly my reaction to it, changed my life completely. The nature of the crisis is not important here, but my reaction to it evolved into a philosophy that works for me to this day. I was forced by some basic instinct of survival to lead myself out of my quandary and eventually find the direction that was missing in my life, primarily by reading about other highly motivated people.

I started my search for answers, and found more questions, which in turn stimulated further searching. Suddenly, I found myself wondering about success—why some people were successful and others were not. I began reading everything I could find on success and positive thinking. Some of the works of Fulton J. Sheen and Andrew Carnegie were excellent starting points. Then, quite coincidentally, a friend gave me a book as a gift. The book was *The Vital Spark* by Lowell Thomas, and it became the strongest influence in my new attitude development. The biographical synopsis of 101 outstanding lives stimulated me to continue searching for the secrets of success. I eventually discovered that success must begin with the realization that each moment in life is a point of no return—we cannot change anything that has happened. This discovery fostered in me the belief that, in order to succeed, one must plan a positive direction in the present to follow into the future. The common "vital spark" which appeared in the lives of the most outstanding persons in world history is the same for all successful people. In the simplest terms it is, "Control your mind and you will control your life." If you can accept this idea, you can begin to develop a positive attitude program that will enhance every aspect of your life.

In terms of your coaching career, remember that people will respond only to challenges and to positive leadership. We cannot force others to do anything they do not want to do. True, it is possible to stimulate people by fear and rewards, but any response will be short-term and inconsistent. The procedures outlined below can help you develop your own positive attitude program for leadership.

First, set aside 30 minutes each day, 5 days a week, for reading books on successful, positive people in any field.

- Analyze their approach to success.
- Isolate the principles that may work for you.
- Inject your own ideas or variations that might make them worth trying.
- Plan how to apply these principles to your own life and career.

Next, at work, at home, or while coaching, begin to apply these principles to your daily life. Keep notes on the things that work, and on the effect they have on you and others. I am sure you will discover, as I have, that the principles of positive attitude are self-regenerating and that the results, both short- and long-term are rewarding. The most immediate, and yet longest lasting, result will be to create a positive self-image for you and in turn for those around you.

Begin your program by reinforcing the positive actions of others. When someone does well, say so. Next, concentrate on developing constructive criticism. If someone makes a mistake, first reinforce the positive part of their effort (no matter how small) before you correct the error. Soon you will begin to notice a gradual change in your attitude. First, your thinking will become positive, and as a result, your actions will become positive. You will realize that you have become a positive person when you suddenly find yourself refusing to give in to a negative idea.

Finally, you must continue to repeat everything—reading, writing, and analyzing—as often as possible. Adjust. Clarify. Let the theme and philosophy of this new "positive attitude" become an integral part of you. This simple, success-oriented program encourages the individual to recognize his or her full potential and to make great strides toward becoming a total, mature leader. It involves a realistic, forward-looking concept, based on the recognition that we can learn from the past, but that we must live in the present and set goals for the future.

Step 3: Proper Use of Time

Nothing in this life is more valuable than time. Each moment, once gone, can never return; every moment squandered can never be replaced. Time is the one thing that everybody will eventually run out of, so we must learn to use it to the fullest. Successful people do not waste time!

And yet, almost everyone, unless specifically trained to plan and organize, wastes too much of it. Proper use of time and planning are inextricably linked. Planning involves both mental and physical activity—both thinking and writing. In order to plan properly, you must write everything down in advance—daily, weekly, monthly, and yearly. Planning develops self-discipline, consistency and a full understanding of the tasks one must perform on a daily basis.

To begin organizing your time, first determine how you use it. For one week, beginning with the first waking moments of every day, record everything that you do. Clock the minutes you spend on each activity (even daydreaming). Also, record the hour that you perform each activity. Include everything—phone calls, interruptions, appointments, meetings, conferences, personal activities, meals, bath-time, and so on. At the end of each day, add up the minutes. You will see then how you have been spending your time.

At the end of the week, review your activity list and underline the standard procedures that you follow every day (eating meals, driving to work, brushing your teeth, etc.). Make a new list of just these items. Next, underline the activities that you perform regularly every day, but that vary in duration (making telephone calls, attending meetings, keeping appointments, engaging in family activities, reading, writing, etc.). Add these items to the new list. Make a list for each activity until you have transferred all of the activities you recorded during the previous week onto one complete list.

This final list should include all the typical demands on your time by your job, your personal life, your civic life, and so on. Each of us has different responsibilities, and therefore different demands on our time. Although it is impossible to present a typical example, the following list may be of help, particularly once you have obtained your head coaching position:

1. Personal Hygiene
2. Meals
3. Commuter Travel
4. Work Preparation
5. Calendar Planning
6. Daily Correspondence
7. Faculty and Student Meetings
8. Business Telephone Calls
9. Organization and Staff Meetings
10. Team Goals and Practice Planning
11. Player Conferences
12. Team Meetings—Motivation and Leadership
13. Film Study
14. Scouting Meetings (information and reports)
15. Individual Player Conferences
16. Fitness Program (season and off-season)
17. League, Conference, and Athletic Department Meetings
18. Personal Fitness and Recreation Activities
19. Personal Goals
20. Family Activities
21. Reading

22. Writing
23. Personal Telephone Calls
24. Civic Activities
25. Interruptions
26. Sleep

Once you have completed the list of all demands on your time, divide your day into three parts—morning, afternoon, and evening. Assign one part of the day for every task, using your original records as a guide for the most appropriate hour. Allow a specific time and number of minutes to complete each task. Refine this plan by experimenting with it for the next few weeks. During this period you will probably discover activities and responsibilities that you did not anticipate. Now you are ready to take charge of your time.

Check your stationery stores for a "daily planner" with the days divided into hour segments (see Figure 1.1 for a sample). Record your priorities each day for one full week. Include enough time for everything, but be sure to allow for surprises, for they are bound to occur. Be flexible; make adjustments daily, as necessary. Eventually you may want to graduate to a self-designed notebook specially suited to your job, your style, and your creativity. You may also find of great help to you the *Coaches Guide to Time Management*, written by Dr. Charles E. Kozoll (1985). This book, published by Human Kinetics Publishers, Inc., is part of the American Coaching Effectiveness Program (ACEP), an educational program widely used throughout the United States, and one that I recommend highly to all aspiring head coaches. The *Coaches Guide to Time Management* is essential reading for any coach wishing to learn how to budget time most effectively.

Good daily preparation makes for good organization and efficiency in your personal and business life. An effectively executed time plan can organize your mind as well as your work, and allow you to become a truly successful individual. You may even find that you are able to accomplish as much as three times the amount of work that you usually accomplish in the course of one day.

Step 4: Goal Planning

Goal planning is to success as scoring more points than your opponent is to victory. A leader must learn how to plan goals from **MARCH 10**

MONDAY, MARCH 10 69/296	TUESDAY, MARCH 11 70/295	WEDNESDAY, MARCH 12 71/294
8 COFFEE - Check Messages	8 COFFEE - Check Messages	8 COFFEE - Check Messages
8:15 Return Important Calls	8:15 Return Important Calls	8:15 Return Important Calls
8:30 FIRST PERIOD P.E.	8:30 FIRST PERIOD P.E.	8:30 FIRST PERIOD P.E.
8:45	8:45	8:45
9	9	9
9:15 OFFICE - phone Calls	9:15 OFFICE - phone Calls	9:15 OFFICE - phone Calls
9:30 Work preparations	9:30 Work Preparations	9:30 Work preparations
9:45	9:45	9:45
10 RECESS - player Confer.	10 RECESS - player Confer.	10 RECESS - player Confer.
10:15 THIRD PERIOD P.E.	10:15 THIRD PERIOD P.E.	10:15 THIRD PERIOD P.E.
10:30	10:30	10:30
10:45	10:45	10:45
11 FOURTH PERIOD HEALTH	11 FOURTH PERIOD HEALTH	11 FOURTH PERIOD HEALTH
11:15	11:15	11:15
11:30	11:30	11:30
11:45 Lunch w/ A.D. @ Ziggs	11:45 Lunch w/ phil H. @ HAMLET	11:45 Lunch w/ ROTARY CLUB
12	12	12
12:15	12:15	12:15
12:30	12:30	12:30
12:45 OFFICE - phone Calls	12:45 OFFICE - phone Calls	12:45 OFFICE - phone Calls
1 Work Preparation	1 Work Preparation	1 Work preparation
1:15	1:15	1:15
1:30 RECESS	1:30 RECESS	1:30 RECESS
1:45 SIXTH PERIOD P.E.	1:45 SIXTH PERIOD P.E.	1:45 SIXTH PERIOD P.E.
2 (Begin off-season	2 (off Season Conditioning)	2 (football team meeting)
2:15 Conditioning program)	2:15	2:15
2:30	2:30	2:30
2:45 Meeting w/ RIDDLE Rep.	2:45 Meeting w/ Team Captains	2:45 Meeting w/ Dean of Athletics
3 Letter to "Scholastic	3	3
3:15 Coach" - Re: Subscript	3:15 Work preparation for	3:15 Work preparation for
3:30 Work preparation for	3:30 Wednesday	3:30 Thursday
3:45 Tuesday	3:45	3:45
4 Sort film for daily	4 FILM STUDY - our offense	4 FILM STUDY - OUR Offen.
4:15 film study this week	4:15 during '85 Season	4:15 during '85 season
4:30	4:30	4:30
4:45	4:45	4:45
5	5	5
5:15	5:15	5:15
5:30 COMMUTE HOME -	5:30 COMMUTE HOME -	5:30 COMMUTE HOME -
5:45 record special notes	5:45 record special notes	5:45 record special notes
6 and observations	6 and observations	6 and observations
6:15	6:15	6:15
6:30	6:30	6:30
6:45	6:45	6:45
7 DINNER @ home	7 DINNER @ home	7 DINNER w/ porters
7:15	7:15	7:15 @ EPICURE
7:30	7:30	7:30
7:45	7:45	7:45
8 Transcribe recorded	8 Transcribe recorded	8 Transcribe recorded
8:15 notes	8:15 notes - prepare speech	8:15 notes
8:30	8:30 for Thursday T.D. CLUB	8:30
8:45	8:45 Meeting	8:45
9	9	9
9:15	9:15	9:15
9:30	9:30	9:30
9:45	9:45	9:45
◄ Clip for Current Week		

Figure 1.1. Sample daily planner.

from **MARCH 13**

THURSDAY, MARCH 13 72/293	FRIDAY, MARCH 14 73/292	SATURDAY, MARCH 15 74/291
8 Coffee - Check Messages	**8** Coffee - Check Messages	**8** Breakfast Meeting w/
8:15 Return Important Calls	8:15 Return Important Calls	8:15 Darryl Smith @ Hamlet
8:30 First Period P.E.	8:30 First Period P.E.	8:30
8:45	8:45	8:45
9	**9**	**9** Football Coaching
9:15 Office - phone Calls	9:15 Office - phone Calls	9:15 Clinic @ Cal State
9:30 Work preparations	9:30 Work preparations	9:30 Northridge
9:45	9:45	9:45
10 Recess - player Confer.	**10** Recess - player Confer.	**10**
10:15 Third Period P.E.	10:15 Third Period P.E.	10:15
10:30	10:30	10:30
10:45	10:45	10:45
11 Fourth Period Health	**11** Fourth Period Health	**11**
11:15	11:15	11:15
11:30	11:30	11:30
11:45 Lunch w/ Mike S. @ Akio's	11:45 Lunch w/ Darryl S. @ Hamlet	11:45
12	**12**	**12**
12:15	12:15	12:15
12:30	12:30	12:30
12:45 Office - phone Calls	12:45 Office - phone Calls	12:45
1 Work preparation	**1** Work preparation	**1**
1:15	1:15	1:15
1:30 Recess	1:30 Recess	1:30
1:45 Sixth Period P.E.	1:45 Sixth Period P.E.	1:45
2 (off-season Conditioning)	**2** (off-season Conditioning)	**2**
2:15	2:15	2:15
2:30	2:30	2:30
2:45 Meeting w/ Coach Lipman	2:45 Meeting w/ Offensive	2:45
3	**3** Coordinator and Key	**3**
3:15 Work preparation for	3:15 offensive Coaches	3:15
3:30 Friday	3:30 to discuss prelim.	3:30
3:45	3:45 ideas for improving	3:45
4 Film Study - our offense	**4** offense for next year	**4**
4:15 during '85 season	4:15	4:15
4:30	4:30	4:30
4:45	4:45	4:45
5	**5**	**5**
5:15	5:15	5:15
5:30 Commute Home -	5:30	5:30
5:45 record special notes	5:45	5:45
6 and observations	**6** Dinner meeting w/	**6** Dinner @ Wildwood
6:15	6:15 offensive Staff @	6:15 and Movie @ UA Theatre
6:30 Transcribe recorded	6:30	6:30
6:45 notes	6:45	**SUNDAY, MARCH 16** 75/290
7 Dinner @ home	**7**	
7:15	7:15	Church - St. Mel's - 10:00
7:30	7:30	
7:45	7:45	Brunch @ Westlake
8 Meeting w/ Touch-	**8**	Plaza Hotel - 12:00
8:15 Down Club (fund	8:15	
8:30 raising plans)	8:30	
8:45	8:45	
9	**9**	
9:15	9:15	
9:30	9:30	
9:45	9:45	

Figure 1.1 Cont.

properly and how to motivate a team to strive for those goals. Before you can learn how to motivate a group of young athletes, you must first develop in yourself the five basic elements that are the foundation of this effort: Desire, Imagination, Courage, Confidence, and Knowledge.

Desire is the product of the fusion of passion and will. It is the embryo from which all ideals emerge, the catalyst that turns existing knowledge into new discovery, dreams into reality, and ideas into action. Nothing of value has ever been and can ever be conceived or accomplished without the passion to conceive it or the will to accomplish it—in short, without desire.

Imagination is the ability to break through the mental and emotional restrictions placed on you by your background and by your own inhibitions. It is a free flow of concepts, ideas, and knowledge that allows you to envision possibilities, and in doing so, develop a plan of action that works toward achievement. Without imagination, little can be accomplished.

Courage is not, as some would have you believe, a lack of fear. It is the ability to overcome fear and to act rationally in the face of it. To be courageous one must first develop tough mental discipline and high moral character. In order to act with courage, you must be steadfast in your beliefs and goals, regardless of outside threats or pressures. You must do what you believe is right.

Confidence is the ability to believe in your ability. It stems from a positive mental attitude, a strong desire, a vivid imagination, and unflinching courage. Confidence allows you to maintain your direction in the face of doubts and ridicule and to remain undeterred by other people's negative attitudes. It is the element that securely bonds a leader and his team as they work toward mutual goals.

Knowledge is a properly balanced blend of information (or facts) and practical experience. In order to work toward a goal you must first fully understand the value of that goal and what is necessary to achieve it. You should be certain that the goals you select are attainable, within the scope of your circumstances, and that you possess sufficient knowledge to achieve them.

Although no plan is perfect, and some may not materialize to your every expectation, I would suggest that you devote considerable time and thought to the planning of your goals.

All goals should fall into one of four categories: ultimate, long-range, medium-range, and short-term. All goals should be team goals. Your ultimate goal is your principle, or overriding, goal. It can be either idealistic or realistic, as long as the preceding goals are capable of being accomplished. The long-range goal may be a few years away from realization but must be obviously realistic. The medium-range goal should be a realistic goal that can be accomplished within a year. The short-term goal must be a goal that you want to attain in a very short time (a week, a month, or two months). While it is essential to have a goal in each category, it is equally essential that you have only one goal in each category. More than one goal will only divert your concentration and cause confusion.

Once your goals have been defined, you must design a plan of action to accomplish each of them. Each plan must be detailed and must spell out your commitment, its elements, the steps necessary to reach the goal, a progress report, and a deadline. The goals must follow in consecutive order. When you have achieved a goal, begin immediately on the next. Once a goal has been reached, do not linger too long, basking in the accomplishment. Move on to the next goal immediately, or you run the danger of regressing.

When you are in the process of setting goals for your team, set them for *your* team only and do not concern yourself with your opponents. Do not worry about what they do, or about what they might do. Concentrate solely on what you must do. The great UCLA basketball coach, John Wooden, has said: "We cannot control what others may do or say, but we can and must control what we do and how we act." Good goal planning improves standards, builds confidence, sharpens perception, eliminates confusion, and increases motivation. It encourages the individual to work well within a team and fosters satisfaction with team accomplishments. In short, it is one more step, an important and basic one, in the "pursuit of excellence."

Step 5: Organization

One of my closest friends, who is also a football coach, frequently remarks to other friends that I am so neat and organized someone could live in the trunk of my car. A slight exaggeration, but fundamentally true. I believe in being organized. I have worked at being organized since my college years. Organization simplifies my life, allows me to deal comprehensively with the unexpected, and makes my recreation worry free. It prepares me for work, helping me to accomplish more in less time. It has helped me to see and take advantage of opportunities and so has made me very lucky—because luck happens when preparation meets opportunity. Organization can also do these things for you.

How can you become organized? If you have started to apply Steps 3 and 4 of this chapter to your life, you have already begun. Now, if we carry this planning to its ultimate conclusion, we can eventually become organized. Organizing is simply the physical act of consolidating a group of elements—systemizing the whole, if you will. The mental part of the process took place when you performed Steps 3 and 4, the planning of your time and goals. There is some thinking involved, naturally, in Step 5, but the art of organization is in finding a place for everything and putting everything in its place. It is good management.

In subsequent chapters we will apply the art of organization to the managing of a high school football program. Chapters 6 through 12 include specific information on how to organize a coaching staff, support staff, facilities, student volunteers, scouting services, practices, parent and booster groups, and so on. My sole purpose in this section, however, is to help you to think and act in an organized fashion.

You can begin by being organized at home. Don't leave your things lying around the house—force yourself all the time to put them in their proper place. Begin this wholesome new life by organizing your clothes closet. Hang your suits in one section, your sports coats in another, your shirts in another, and so on. If you do not already have one, purchase a shoe rack and lay your shoes out in pairs so they are easy to find. Neatly organize your dresser drawers, your bathroom cabinets, your hobby area or work bench.

Using an extra bedroom, or just a desk in the corner of the living room or family room, set up an office area—a place you can use to do all the work that you need to do at home. Make this area your exclusive work area and organize it thoroughly with proper lighting, adequate supplies (pencils, pens, pads, paper, erasers), concise and accurate files, compartmentalized drawers, desk top organizers, and so forth. Make sure that you have a comfortable chair on which to work, a telephone, a pencil sharpener, and if you type, a typewriter. Use this area whenever you work at home and always keep it neat.

Next, get a good, compartmentalized briefcase. Always carry it with you between your office and your home and at any other times when you think you might need it. Keep in it at all times your daily planner, address book, player and staff rosters, pens, pencils, note pads, rule book, and file folders for important papers. You may also want to keep personal accessories in it (i.e., eye glasses, calculator, recorder, checkbook) for your convenience, but do not throw things into your briefcase haphazardly. Put everything into compartments and, as often as possible, in the same place. I have seen briefcases that looked too dangerous to reach into for fear of losing an arm to some unseen creature lurking behind the mess inside. This kind of briefcase will not help your quest for organization.

Once you have begun to develop the feel for organization at home, you can also begin to organize your office away from home. Try to organize your desk and files in the same manner that you organized your home office area. Put everything in the same place on both desks and keep the same accessories in the same drawers. Maintain accurate files in both places—the office files, particularly relating to staff and player personnel, must be meticulously complete, while the home files should be a more concise, less detailed version. All available data relating to personnel must be kept in individual file folders and secured in a locked file cabinet.

Your final exercise in the search for an orderly existence lies in observation. During your normal, everyday activities, look for things that are improperly placed. If you can control and correct these things, then do so; if not, make a mental note of them for your own future reference. Finally, I would like you to keep in mind that you are not working to become organized just for the sake of saying you are organized. You are, in the meantime, developing a knowledge of, and an instinct for, organization so that you may help yourself and others in your program to perform at their highest levels.

Step 6: Motivation and Discipline

Motivation and discipline are integral parts of teaching and learning. They are essential elements of leadership. A leader must be able to motivate others, and must understand the basic human concepts behind discipline. The ability to motivate might be defined as the ability to show people their goals and their potential. Discipline is the systematic training for, or subjection to, an ultimate goal.

Motivation is not simply the ability to make fiery speeches before a game or at the half. It is not gimmickry or canned oratory. Motivation is a magic that results from day-in and day-out working. It is not logical to ask an athlete to search inside himself for something extra to give, when you've failed to reach him before that time. Every coach must emphasize the kind of positive motivation that stimulates maximum effort and develops pride and confidence. For a leader to be able to motivate others he must first be able to motivate himself. Motivation cannot be taken for granted, or worked on only occasionally. It cannot be contrived but must come from steady work and planning. It begins with the role models you gather around you, your assistant coaches for instance, and with the way you handle yourself and the way you organize practices. If your practices are properly organized and disciplined, and your coaches are well prepared, your players will respect both you and your staff. And that is the most important thing you can do before motivating anyone—you must earn respect.

Respect generates respect. We must understand that we are dealing with boys, and that we are making mental and physical demands on them that may be difficult even for men to meet. Each young man has his own emotions and his own reactions to everything. Youngsters between 14 and 18 are growing and changing from year to year, from week to week, from day to day, and from hour to hour. Your effort to understand them will be directly related to their ability to respect you. Your players will learn to understand you if you have a true desire to accomplish something, and find it easy to be yourself. If your own genuine excitement can create an environment that is conducive to enthusiasm, and if your coaching staff is comprised of good teachers who take time to work with the young men, the players will motivate themselves. True motivation comes from within, and if a player feels that a coach can make a contribution, he will listen.

Coaches should not worry so much about creating motivation as they should about destroying it. Too often coaches spend too much time motivating the team and not enough time motivating individuals to strive for team goals. The key to motivating a team lies in your ability to convince each player that you are interested in his development both as an athlete and a human being. If you can do this, the player will do anything for you. Remember the five *D* principles, when you work on developing your ability to motivate others: Direction, Desire, Dedication, Determination, and Discipline. You must select the *direction* that will ultimately lead you to your goals. You must truly *desire* whatever you are trying to accomplish. You must be *dedicated* to the pursuit of excellence in order to accomplish your desired goals. You must be *determined* in your resolve and strong in your ability to withstand all challenges. You must have the *discipline* to sacrifice in order to maintain steady progress toward your goals. Working on these principles will help make you the kind of leader who says "Follow me," not the kind who says, "Get going." This is the kind of leader who motivates others.

Discipline is an area that has gotten more coaches into trouble than any other area. Many coaches, particularly young ones, think that they have to be iron fisted to prevent their athletes from taking advantage of them. They believe that berating players by yelling and screaming at them is the criterion used to measure a "tough coach." But discipline is a double-edged sword. If it is not wielded with skill and control, it can cut in both directions. The personality of the individual has a lot to do with one's approach to discipline. Some coaches can be dictators and others more fatherly, but regardless of the approach, the good coach must understand that firmness *and* fairness are the most essential ingredients for being a strong leader.

The basic elements of proper discipline are punishment and reward. Then why do so many coaches feel that only punishment applies to discipline? Probably because they use discipline to reinforce their own egos and not for the best interests of the team. Some coaches make so many rules for discipline that their players begin to think of them as adversaries. This type of coach usually talks about his players as if they were the enemy rather than partners in a joint effort. And, most predictably, he blames losing seasons on the players, never on himself. These "coaches" will never be leaders, and threats of whips, chains, or alligator pits will never instill real discipline in their players. The genuinely tough coach has few rules for discipline.

The secret to proper discipline is to keep the rules relating to disciplinary action simple and few. They should be rules with a broad view, such as, "Never disgrace the team or the school," and the punishment should be commensurate with the degree of the violation. On the other hand, those who never violate the rules should be rewarded by special recognition or awards for their own discipline. Therein lies the key: All disciplinary rules should aim towards developing self-discipline in players. The more players you can help to become self-disciplined, the more successful your program will be. Conversely, all failures have one thing in common—lack of discipline!

Finally, there is one characteristic of a coach that is absolutely necessary to avoid disciplinary breakdown, and that is confidence. The more confident you are, as a result of solid preparation, the less you will resent challenges to your authority. The more you have the players' trust and confidence, the less often you will be challenged or questioned. If you create an atmosphere of mistrust and resentment, your players may not question or challenge you to your face—but don't eavesdrop in the locker room!!!

Step 7: Accepting Challenge

Life is full of little challenges that we face every day. Just making a decent living these days is challenge enough for most people. However, if you want to be successful in the coaching field you must challenge yourself beyond the norm. Coaching is a high-stress occupation that exacts hard work, often long hours, and always mental, physical, and emotional demands rarely asked of other professions. The great Vince Lombardi wrote "Leadership is in sacrifice, is in self-denial. It is in love, it is in fearlessness. It is in humility and it is in the perfectly disciplined will. This is also the distinction between great and little men." Coaching offers you the challenge of greatness as few other professions can. In order to achieve this greatness you must continually challenge yourself to improve, to learn, to communicate, to lead, to inspire, and to give of yourself. You must constantly strive to develop the instinct for recognizing excellence, and then you must pursue it relentlessly.

Steps 1 through 6 of this chapter comprise your first challenge. When you can evaluate yourself honestly, develop a positive attitude, use your time properly, plan your goals, organize your life, learn to motivate others, and understand the concepts of discipline, you will have taken your first step towards success. This initial challenge and all subsequent challenges require three basic abilities, all three of which anyone can develop in a relatively short time.

- *Concentration*. You must develop your ability to concentrate on the challenge before you. Shut out distractions and see the total demand and its resolution. Most successful people are those with extraordinary concentration.
- *Patience.* There is almost no problem that patience cannot solve. You are never defeated until you lose your patience. Simply continue to work until the challenge is overcome and eventually you will be successful.
- *Relaxation.* A truly great leader must learn the art of relaxation. Tension not only hampers creativity, imagination, and the logical thought process, doctors now agree that it can kill!

If you need to work on developing these abilities, ask your local librarian to recommend some good books on these subjects, or check your favorite video store to select some videocassettes from the abundance of material now available.

Preparing yourself for leadership will not be a casual task; it is a most formidable challenge. However, the end result will be fulfilling and unendingly beneficial to your career as a coach. Leadership is the art of getting things accomplished through others. The seven steps outlined in this chapter will help you to acquire the ability to convey an attitude that instills others with confidence. They will help you to develop poise and self-assurance that will call forth the respect, admiration, and best efforts of your staff and players. They will also help you to work on all of the qualities required of a good leader, including honesty, integrity, patience, intelligence, knowledge, communication, trust, and confidence—the basic elements that are essential to true success. Knowledge of this truth, combined with the efforts you make in preparing yourself for leadership, will put you on the right track toward the pursuit of excellence.

Chapter 2

Developing a Coaching Philosophy

A coaching philosophy is a system of principles that will regulate your approach and conduct while you build your football program. It is a fundamental doctrine of behavior that must reflect your own personality. Your ability to perform as a leader and coach is relative to your developing a coaching philosophy that mirrors your style, ethics, logic, and creativity. A head coach, or any coach for that matter, must be true to himself. He must always function within a philosophy that maintains his integrity.

Two Major Decisions

There are certain decisions that will be necessary for you to make before you can develop a coaching philosophy that reflects your own beliefs. First, you will need to decide just what your coaching style will be. By the time you reach the point in your career where you are qualified to assume a high school head coaching position, you will probably have established a style that you feel comfortable with. The chances are that it will fall into one of two categories: dictatorship or democracy. In the dictatorship system, the head coach makes all the decisions and the assistant coaches and players follow precise orders without deviation. Everything is done the head coach's way, with military-like obedience. This is a style of coaching that has worked, and does work for some coaches, but it demands an enormous commitment of time and effort as well as an inordinate amount of knowledge of the game. You will not be successful in this style unless you possess this commitment and this knowledge, plus the charisma to carry it off. In the democratic system, the head coach is the leader of a cooperative effort. He solicits creative input from his assistant coaches and from his players. The head coach is ultimately responsible for making major decisions, but the democratic style more equally shares the burdens of time, effort, and knowledge among all those participating in the team effort.

Which style of coaching works for you? Do not base your decision on what has worked for others. Young coaches often try to imitate a famous or former coach that they admire, but this can cause problems with credibility. You must emphasize your own style—one that will be consistent with your own personality.

The second decision that you need to make is the priorities you wish to emphasize in your program. You should clearly define the importance you want to place on winning, development of your players, and enjoyment of the game. These are the three major areas of emphasis in coaching any sport. *Coaching Young Athletes* (Martens, Christina, Harvey, & Sharkey, 1981) has an excellent chapter on coaching objectives that I consider required reading for anyone who wishes to develop a solid coaching philosophy. This book will help you understand the ramifications of selecting certain priorities and will clarify criteria that are essential for making valid decisions about your own coaching philosophy.

Many factors need to be addressed within the framework of these two major decisions. I would like to express some of those considerations here and indicate some of their specific benefits.

Overall Player Development

When developing a coaching philosophy in any sport, the primary consideration should be the welfare and development of your players. Your success depends on their effort, and their effort is directly related to how much they feel you care about them. Imagine if you will that your star player, a seventeen-year-old quarterback in the throes of an emotional adolescent crisis, comes to you for counsel. If you should ignore or patronize him, he will feel as though you let him down, and he will consequently never be concerned about letting you down. If, on the other hand, you show genuine interest and offer some mature guidance, his faith in your concern for his welfare may help him to maintain focus on his other responsibilities—to his teammates and his coaches.

Directly related to the development of your players is the teaching of positive personal values through the football coaching process. If you wish your players to develop winning attitudes, it is important that you first instill within them certain basic values, such as honesty, desire, determination, leadership, aggressiveness, self-confidence, emotional control, mental toughness, trustworthiness, and the ability to accept responsibility. These things can be taught only by example and by constant reinforcement of positive action. The more successful you and your staff are in teaching these values to your players, the faster you will be able to accomplish your goals. Your players' respect for you will grow, because they will know that you are working to help them. They will begin to discipline and motivate themselves to accomplish the team goals that you have set for them.

Since football is a game that is played as much from the eyebrows up as from the shoulderpads down, it is incumbent upon you as the head coach to work as hard on cultivating your players' minds as you do on developing their bodies. You must encourage them at all times in their pursuit of academic excellence. You may even find it necessary to devote some time to the instruction of proper study techniques and good study habits. Remember, a smart player with average talent is usually better, and always more consistent, than an ignorant player with great talent. Smart players make fewer mistakes, learn faster, are generally well prepared, and tend to handle critical situations better. They are usually self-motivated and self-disciplined. Only a smart player can develop into a leader, and leadership is necessary for success.

General Philosophy

Academicians often consider "winning" to be an evil concept. They tend to associate winning with cheating and with the "win at all costs" mentality of the often well-publicized morons (masquerading as coaches) who pursue victory at the expense of their players' well-being. To be a true leader in your profession you must do your best to dispel this ugly stereotype. Your conduct as an honest, ethical head coach who never breaks the rules and who genuinely cares for the well-being of his athletes will go a long way toward accomplishing this end. The result, in all probability, will be a winning program with no need to apologize for your desire to win—for to be a successful head coach you *must* have a strong desire to win. Making your best effort to win is an essential part of competition. If you do not strive to win, there really is no valid reason to compete. The emphasis that you place on winning should be more accurately directed to "always making your best effort" to win. Your desire to win must be for *us* to win, not for *me* to win—you are, after all, the leader of a team effort. But you must also make sure that you never blame defeat on anyone but yourself. You, as head coach, should have the maturity to accept any blame that accompanies a loss. Conversely, the plaudits for victory should be generously given to your players and your staff as an indication of your appreciation for their hard work.

In chapter 1 we discussed the role that proper goal planning plays in building a successful football program. It will be necessary for you to communicate the relationship between goal planning and success to your staff and players. Goals must be set at all levels in the program, so you should encourage everyone in your program to develop personal goals while keeping in mind that all individual goals must be consistent with team goals. The rewards for this effort will amaze you. Short-term team goals will be achieved faster and more completely than you could ever anticipate—which will allow the team to pursue medium-range goals sooner and with greater enthusiasm.

You will remember that in chapter 1 I mentioned the necessity for you to confront such issues as morality, jeopardy, and responsibility. These issues should be major considerations in developing your coaching philosophy, particularly in that you have both a moral and a legal responsibility to safeguard the health and well-being of your athletes. You need to develop a fundamental understanding of sports science and sports medicine. Many city hospitals with orthopedic departments that deal with sports-related injuries often hold clinics or symposiums on sports medicine. There are also many books and magazine articles listed in the bibliography of this book that are directed specifically towards laypeople. I suggest that you start working on this phase of your coaching education immediately. To become a consistent winner the head coach must understand the physical and emotional individuality of his players and the dynamics of group interaction. This knowledge must be incorporated into your philosophy in a manner that is consistent with your coaching style.

The general principles that you wish to use in motivating and disciplining your players should also be incorporated into your coaching philosophy. The self-motivated and self-disciplined person tends to accept a challenge in stride and, as a result, will most likely prevail. The ultimate achievement for a head coach is to be so effective in his approach to developing self-motivation and self-discipline in his athletes that he rarely ever need impose his will upon them for this purpose.

Playing Philosophy

Once you have secured a head coaching position, there will most certainly be a need to develop a philosophy about the way you desire to play the game. Since this book will not be dealing with the specifics of Xs and Os, I will simply touch upon a few general rules for your consideration while you are working on your own playing philosophy:

- Be sure that your approach to the game reflects your own personality and style and is consistent with what you truly believe.

- Before you develop specifics of your game, consider the type of athletes that you expect to have in your program on a regular basis to insure the probability of its successful execution.
- Analyze your talent on a yearly basis so you can adjust the specifics of your game to take full advantage of that talent.
- Develop a master playbook which should be a complete catalog of your entire offense, defense, and kicking game, including all variations required for yearly adjustments.
- Develop a "signature" for your program. This should be a phase of the game that you will place great emphasis on perfecting. It must be an extra dimension with which your program can build a positive reputation year after year (extremely hard hitting, mistake-free football, an unstoppable inside short running game, etc.).

These considerations, together with the recommended research, should help you to outline your own coaching philosophy. As an additional cross-check, while you are detailing the specifics of the philosophy on which your program will be based, you might wish to compare your anticipated results with the following maxims of coaching philosophy:

Coaches With Sound Philosophies Will

- Know thyself.
- Think "we," not "me."
- Never alibi or make excuses.
- Disdain self-pity.
- Teach first, coach after.
- Believe in your players and your coaches.
- Be a good technician.
- Pay infinite attention to infinitesimal details.
- Rely on your own abilities.
- Create attitude, not rules.
- Treat your coaches and players with respect.
- Avoid favoritism.
- Be a man of your word.

Programs Based Upon a Sound Philosophy Will

- Be dynamic and innovative.
- Foster pride through tradition.

- Develop men, not just players.
- Teach a positive work ethic.
- Instill the players with "the magic of believing."
- Recognize the rights of the individual while developing a group instinct.
- Develop consistency.
- Develop a feeling of camaraderie and a sense of security for the players.
- Reinforce a desire for achievement and underscore the satisfaction of accomplishment.
- Obtain recognition for the athletes.
- Help the athletes develop self-esteem.
- Promote the invitation of challenges.

These maxims are general goals that most coaches agree must be the aim of any good coaching philosophy. Notwithstanding the fact that it is necessary for each of us to formulate an individual coaching philosophy, there are also two fundamental DOs and one basic DON'T that are imperative. DO develop an understanding and an empathy with the athletes that will allow you to be capable of forgiveness. DO demonstrate firmness and the ability to discipline when necessary. DON'T create a philosophy that will subordinate the interests of the team, or of your assistant coaches, to your own.

It might be wise not to chisel your initial coaching philosophy onto stone tablets. Leave yourself some room to maneuver. For the first few years you will probably find a need to adjust or to amend your approach. Try not to force yourself into a tight corner that you cannot get out of without looking like a first-class idiot!

Chapter 3

Seeking the Job— and Getting It

New Self-Appraisal

Aphenomenon that has remained a mystery to me throughout all of my years in business and coaching is that it is always easier to secure another position when you are employed than when you are unemployed. Unless it is unavoidable, one should not resign one's job without having secured another position. However, it is a good policy to advise your present employer that you will be making inquiries about available head coaching positions, if this can be done without compromising your present job.

During my tenure as a business executive, prior to entering coaching, I was involved in the employment process to a considerable extent. Numerous times well-qualified candidates applying for positions were overlooked or given less than serious consideration due to an incomplete or poorly prepared résumé. Others lost employment opportunities because they lacked confidence and failed to sell themselves or their qualifications in face-to-face interviews. For the prospective head coach to prime himself for the opportunity to move upward, he must first prepare himself to convince prospective employers that he possesses the most and the best of what they are seeking. It is essential that he be able to do this both in writing and in conversation. The initial approach to this preparation is to recall the self-evaluation you performed in chapter 1, step 1. Pay particular attention to the material with regard to where you are now and what you have to offer a program as head coach.

Review your questions and do a new self-appraisal with new, in-depth answers. Using this second appraisal, write a positive essay on your self-image as a head coach. Begin by building on your strengths and assets while acknowledging your weaknesses with a clear-cut program for overcoming them. The object of this exercise is to help you focus clearly on realities. Do not approach the exercise as if you were writing a press release. Be positive, but honest. Continue to rework and refine your essay until you are truly able to say, "This is really me and these are the positive elements that I have to offer as a head coach."

A Proper Résumé

When you reach this point you will have developed sufficient confidence to create a well-conceived résumé. Although a résumé is a summary of your background, it should be a complete summary and not a sketchy one- or two-page listing of your previous jobs. The most impressive résumés that I have seen were several pages long (some were bound) and contained thorough background information on education, past employment, activities, honors, club affiliations, and so on. A good résumé, in my opinion, is an entire personal background presented in a concise, easy-to-read form.

A proper résumé for an aspiring head football coach should be constructed in the following manner:

Front Cover Page—Heavyweight paper of a light color (gray, tan, light blue) with black ink. "RÉSUMÉ OF (Your Name)" centered on page in uppercase letters. Month and year the résumé is issued on lower right of page.

First Page—Standard white bond with black ink. All personal information such as name, current address, home and business telephone numbers, credential and certification information, and present employer's name and address neatly spaced and centered. Indicate whether or not your present employer may be contacted.

Second Page—Divider page. Standard white bond with black ink. "EDUCATIONAL BACKGROUND" centered on page in uppercase letters.

Third Page—Standard white bond with black ink. A complete account of your secondary school education, including name and address of your high school, date of your graduation, type of diploma (if specified), overall grade point average, class standing at graduation, academic honors, honor societies, clubs and extra curricular activities neatly spaced and centered. (You may omit certain entries that are not consistent with, or relative to, your overall education.)

Fourth Page—Standard white bond with black ink. An overall view of your undergraduate college education, including name and address of your college, degree obtained, major course of study, minor course(s) of study, date of graduation, graduation honors (magna cum laude, summa cum laude, cum laude) or class standing at graduation, other academic honors or societies, clubs and extra-curricular activities neatly spaced and centered. If accreditation or certification was received at this level, state specifics.

Fifth Page—Standard white bond with black ink. A complete record of your postgraduate study, including the name(s) and address(es) of the graduate school(s) you have attended, the degree(s) you have obtained, the years attended, date(s) of completion neatly spaced and centered. Indicate all academic honors received or honor society inductions. If accreditation or certification was received at this level, state specifics.

Sixth Page—Divider page. Standard white bond with black ink. "ATHLETIC BACKGROUND" centered in uppercase letters.

Seventh Page—Standard white bond with black ink. An itemized list of the sports you have played starting with your first year of athletics in high school, on a year-by-year basis. (Be specific: varsity football, J.V. baseball, etc.) Footnote any awards or honors you received during high school. Then repeat this format for college and, if applicable, professional sports.

Eighth Page—Divider page. Standard white bond with black ink. "EMPLOYMENT BACKGROUND" centered on page in uppercase letters.

Ninth Page—Standard white bond with black ink. Your work history from first coaching assignment to present position, neatly spaced and centered, as follows:

FROM   TO   EMPLOYER   POSITION(S) REASON FOR LEAVING
(month & year) (name & address)   (itemized)   (brief)

Include teaching assignments (subjects), additional sports coaching, and administrative duties. State your reason for leaving briefly and concisely.

Tenth Page—Divider page. Standard white bond with black ink. "REFERENCES" centered on page in uppercase letters.

Eleventh Page—Standard white bond with black ink. A list of five personal references on the top half of the page, and a list of five business references on the bottom half of the page, neatly spaced and centered. With each reference, include a complete address and telephone number. With each business reference, also include the person's position or title and your working relationship.

Back Cover Page—Heavyweight paper to match front cover. Nothing imprinted. Bind into book with black plastic loop or spiral binding.

Take great pains with word choice, and meticulously check your spelling. Your résumé can be an outstanding personal presentation that will call immediate attention to your thoroughness, confidence, and ability to organize, as well as provide a complete, concise, and easy-to-read account of your total background as it relates to the job for which you are applying.

Apply for the Right Jobs

The next step is to find the proper positions to apply for. Do not delude yourself into believing that any head coaching position is good for a start. Many a young coach has made the mistake of taking a head coaching job at a school that was ill suited to his personality or coaching philosophy, only to find himself unable to develop the type of program he believes in, and often leading to disastrous results. Sometimes accepting the wrong job can adversely affect a young coach's career for many years. There are times when you will benefit more by turning down a position than by accepting it, perhaps even developing a better insight into the kind of position you require.

There are many factors to consider in determining a person-job match. Job listings and advertisements for available positions are easily obtainable: Coaching periodicals regularly run advertisements. National, regional, and local coaches' associations print lists and newsletters with job leads, and coaching clinics usually have similar information available. You should take advantage of this plethora of information and write as many inquiry letters as you can.

In your inquiry letter you should indicate your interest in the job, ask any questions you might have about it, and briefly describe your present position. Follow up on these letters of inquiry with a telephone call approximately ten days to two weeks later. If by that time the school has indicated an interest in you and you feel that the response to your inquiry was positive and encouraging, you should send a résumé. Do not send your résumé before you have made initial contact and are satisfied that there is some mutual interest. It is always good psychology to keep a prospective employer's interest piqued—first an interesting letter, then a personable telephone call, then an overwhelming résumé. Finally, the self-appraisal you have worked on will instill within you the confidence to conduct a relaxed and poised interview.

The Interview—a Two-Way Street

An interview is a two-way street—you must find out about the interviewers, too. It is important during the interview to ask key questions on matters that concern you. Do not be arrogant, but indicate your interest in the mutual benefit of this possible alliance. Subtly acquire as much information as you can from an interview, and set up as many interviews with as many different places as possible. Analyze the information you have gathered; then focus on the two or three positions that are most suited to you. Remember, too, that there are ways other than the interview to garner information about a prospective employer —in telephone conversations, through casual conversation with other coaches or teachers, from research while on campus for an interview. The following section contains some questions you should be able to answer, and explains some of the areas that should be investigated before you accept an offer at any high school.

Consider the Offers

Do you know the circumstances that led to the school's search for a new head football coach? In order for you to determine how secure your own position will be, it would be wise to find out if the previous head coach was fired, resigned, or retired—and why. This will help give you some insight into the kind of program that the former head coach developed, as well as the criteria used by the administration for judging the capabilities of the head football coach.

Do you know anything about the football program's budget allowance? Budget will have a strong effect on your ability to build a good program. The hiring of assistant coaches and support staff, and the purchase of proper supplies and equipment are all contingent upon the budget. If the school-funded budget is not sufficient to support a quality program, then it will require additional private financing. You will need to find out what type of outside fund-raising activities are available to you and what the administration policies and regulations are with regard to the distribution of funds raised by the football program. Find out specifically if your program would be able to use all of the funds it can raise from outside fund-raising activities.

What are the policies of the administration and athletic director regarding the hiring of assistant coaches, trainers, and so on? It would be helpful to know if some restrictions might keep you from selecting the staff of your choice. For instance, if all of your staff had to be teachers, or if the number of paid assistants you could have was limited, or if you were not permitted to use students for your support staff, your ability to function as an effective head coach might be impaired.

What do you know about the former head coach? Was he a "legend" beloved by everyone, who retired after having developed and guided a highly successful, winning program at that school for several years? If so, then the task of establishing your own successful image can be Herculean.

Do you know if the administration truly supports the school's football program? If the administration does not believe that sports in general and football in particular have any value as teaching tools, the program will be subjected to constant negative input from the highest level.

These five areas require thorough investigation and careful evaluation prior to accepting any head coaching position. However, the "kiss of death" to a new head coach can lie waiting for him in the last two areas—following a "legend" and working for administrators who consider football, at best, "a necessary evil." To function and pursue your goal of excellence in the face of these negative pressures takes a measure of dedication and determination that few men possess. To briefly illustrate the overwhelming effect that these situations can have on a program, I shall cite one famous example and one personal experience.

The great former UCLA basketball coach John Wooden, truly a legend in his own time, retired as the most successful college basketball coach of all time. He was beloved by players, fans, and the press alike, and was generally considered a coaching genius. The man who replaced him as head basketball coach for the UCLA Bruins was Gene Bartow. Bartow was, in his own right, an excellent basketball coach and had an outstanding record at UCLA. However, he was not John Wooden, nor did he ever try to be. But the fans and the press were never satisfied with his efforts, which were monumental in the face of such pressure; and they badgered and belittled him even on a personal level. Eventually Coach Bartow resigned in favor of another coaching position and, naturally, is now quite successful and well respected. Four other well-qualified, exceptional coaches, most maintaining excellent records, have headed the basketball program at UCLA in almost a decade since John Wooden retired. To this day they cannot escape comparison with him. There are many instances of a similar nature occurring in football, too: Vince Lombardi at Green Bay, Paul "Bear" Bryant at Alabama, Ara Parseghian at Notre Dame, and so on. The unjustified criticism has little to do with the ability of the men replacing them. There is simply an overwhelming negative aura that envelops an entire program in such cases—an aura that stifles the ability of most men to instill a positive atmosphere in which to build their own program.

Several years ago, when I was working as a defensive coordinator in a high school program, I had a discussion with the dean of athletics, at his request, about the problems within the football program. The discussion centered on the growing discontent bordering on mutiny that involved the players and their parents. Because I had already notified the administration that I would be leaving to take another position, the dean of athletics asked me if I could shed some light on the cause of these problems. The focus of the controversy centered, naturally, on the head football coach, although the fault was not entirely his. True, the head coach is ultimately responsible for the performance of his team, and this particular coach was not fully prepared for this assignment when he accepted the position. However, the school administration played a major role in the failure of this program. With the possible exception of the dean of athletics, with whom I had the meeting, the school administrators (including the athletic director, oddly enough) considered the football program to have no real value in the educational process; they believed that it distracted from a true education, and so the program was barely tolerated as a necessary evil. This negativism created a "who cares" attitude, first within the faculty, then within the student body, and eventually among the players themselves. The head football coach was unable to reverse this negative wave and, as a result, the program failed.

I discussed these observations with a very shocked dean of athletics. He thanked me for my honesty and said that he would make an effort to reverse this trend, but he left that school the following year for reasons which are unknown to me. The head coach, who was determined to develop a successful program, made great strides in his personal and professional development, and he worked diligently to turn the program around. His efforts were fruitless, however, until the school administrators were replaced by administrators who believed in a solid athletic program. Almost instantly the football program turned around and finally met with measurable success.

Some people claim that a strong will can conquer any challenge, and I agree. My concern, however, is that few of us have the kind of inner strength and charisma necessary to over-come these two particular threats. My personal advice is to avoid these situations if at all possible. Building an excellent high school football program is sufficient challenge in itself. There is no need to impede your progress with a built-in death wish!

Chapter 4

Establishing Your Program

I n order to establish a solid foundation for your
program, it is essential that you start your new
assignment no later than the beginning of the
spring semester (January-February) prior to your
first football season. Both you and the school administrators
should understand that postponement beyond this point will
only delay the proper development of the program. The timing
used in this chapter is based upon the premise that your new
job will start no later than the first week in February, and that
you will be notified that you have the job at least two weeks prior
to starting.

Select a Conditioning Coach

Immediately after you have accepted the position of a head
football coach, you should locate a qualified conditioning coach.
It is advisable that he be an accredited teacher and someone with
whom you have had a previous association, or know at least by
reputation. He should be mature, knowledgeable in the field of

strength training and exercise, reliable, and completely responsible—someone who you feel totally confident will care for and teach your young men to prepare their bodies for the rigors of a demanding season.

You will be spending extremely long hours with this conditioning coach before starting your new job. First you need to develop a complete conditioning/strength program designed specifically for the high school football player. Next, you will need a plan for implementing this program so that you can properly incorporate it into your overall schedule for the off-season, preseason, and season. And, finally, you must draft a list of recommendations for changing and/or improving the weight room to meet your specific needs. I also strongly urge that before you finalize your conditioning/strength program you send for a copy of *A Coach's Guide to Safe Football* prepared by Bill Murray and Dick Herbert for the American Football Coaches Association. This book provides valuable expert medical advice on safety and conditioning. The information it contains, supplemented with the suggested readings in sports science and sports medicine in the bibliography, will assist you in developing a safe and effective conditioning/strength program.

Meet With the Athletic Director

Your first order of business once you have started your new job should be to schedule a meeting with the athletic director. Prepare your own agenda for this meeting, which should include (a) visual inspection of all playing and practice facilities, equipment, and supplies, (b) inspection of the weight room, (c) discussion of the circumstances under which the previous head coach left, (d) review of the fall football schedule and discussion of opponents with particular regard to open dates, (e) in-depth discussion of your budget and possible supplemental fundraising activities, (f) obtaining a comprehensive list of all the football players currently in your program at all levels (roster lists, game programs, etc.), (g) requesting unrestricted use of all game films and a projector, and (h) a thorough discussion of your new ideas, plans and programs for the off-season, preseason, and season.

In preparing your agenda for this meeting, you should be ready to give your own views in each of these areas. After inspecting the playing facilities, practice facilities, equipment, supplies, and weight room, make notes on the condition that they are in as you discuss them with the athletic director. Ask specific questions about any possible resentment that may be lingering as a result of the previous head coach leaving. You must be very straightforward in your views about participating in the selection of opposing teams. If there are any remaining open dates on your upcoming first season schedule, you should request the prerogative of choosing these opponents from those that are available. You should maintain the right to approve all future scheduling prior to confirmation. It is also very important that you make every effort to see that as many games as possible are scheduled on Friday evenings. This will allow for the proper blend of practice time, meetings, scouting analysis, and relaxation, all of which will be discussed in detail in chapters 9 and 10.

Be prepared, while discussing the budget, to present the anticipated cost of staffing and operating your program for the first season. These figures will undoubtedly be considerably higher than the school budget allows, and might send the athletic director into shock. However, if you follow your presentation of these costs with some solid suggestions on outside fund-raising activities (e.g., Las Vegas Night, 10K runs, candy sales) you will keep him from a coronary and will probably even elicit his help in organizing some of these activities.

This meeting will be your best opportunity to ask for complete athletic, academic, and medical information on all the athletes in your program. You will also want to request at this time all game films or tapes and the exclusive use of a high-quality coaching projector or video recorder, as well as a room to be used for film viewing and storage. Finally, you must be prepared to discuss in depth your new ideas for the football program, including the ability of your conditioning coach to function as a teacher, if required; your plans and schedules of activities for the off-season, preseason, and season; and the type of cooperation you wish to foster among the administration, faculty, and student body. You should probably include in this discussion your plans for some visible improvements before the season (new helmets, new jerseys, improved playing facilities, etc.). At least one such improvement made before each season is symbolic of positive change, and tends to foster pride within the football family as well as interest in the football program among the faculty and students.

Immediately after this comprehensive meeting with the athletic director you should sit down and organize your notes on each subject. Write down exactly what was discussed and what decisions were made. The next day, type a memo to the athletic director including all this information and any additional recommendations or suggestions you might have. Keep a copy in your files and stay abreast of the progress in these areas for your next meeting with the athletic director.

Begin Basic Conditioning Program

Schedule a general meeting for all returning football players at all levels, and send a personally addressed notice to each player. If you are in a school that schedules a last-period P.E. class for interscholastic athletics, you might use that time for the meeting. Because many high schools throughout the country do allow a last-period P.E. class for major sports, all the scheduling in this book will be based on that format. If your school does not offer that bonus period, simply assume that the meeting scheduled for this time will be held immediately after school.

At this players' meeting you should be prepared to introduce yourself and your conditioning coach, briefly explain your program (with some insight into your coaching philosophy), and present the compulsory varsity off-season conditioning/strength program, which should start the very next day. Also inform the players at this meeting that you will be scheduling interviews with each one of them during the off-season, and tell them some of the topics you will be discussing in these interviews so that they can prepare. The basic off-season conditioning/strength program, at this point, should be a three-day weight workout and two-day flexibility and stretching workout, with emphasis on upper body strength and lower body flexibility. Your conditioning coach should tend to the details, scheduling, and supervising of the program, with your approval, while you concentrate on preparing for and conducting the individual player interviews.

The reason for selecting a conditioning coach with a P.E. teaching credential is to obviate any problems in having him conduct a last-period P.E. class.

Conduct Player Interviews

As soon as you have received all the player personnel information that you requested from the athletic director, you can begin to evaluate your players. Watch and rewatch every returning player. Evaluate, grade, examine, and visualize each athlete in terms of your new system. Make notes, comments, questions—write everything down! Take additional time to watch these young men in physical education classes and other sports in which they participate. Watch how they move and further evaluate their athletic ability. Make more notes! This will help you to accomplish two other very important functions: observe other athletes who have, until now, chosen not to participate in football, and establish yourself as a supporter of coaches in other sports. Once you have satisfied yourself that you know your players athletically, you must get to know them academically. Make appointments with the school counselors to obtain basic information. Essentially, you require general information only on their grade point averages, problem subjects, best subjects, and any disciplinary problems or conflicts with teachers that they may have. Give the counselors a simple, xeroxed form to fill out that contains space for all this information. Be sure to acquire a current class schedule for each young man, and use these schedules to start individual files on each player.

You are now ready to conduct your personal interviews. Contact each young man and decide on a time that is convenient for both of you, allowing at least twenty minutes for an interview. Start each interview by asking the student if he has enjoyed playing football; find out what he likes about it and what he doesn't. Ask him how he feels about his performance last year, and what he would like to accomplish this year. Discuss your evaluation of his past performance, first the good qualities, then the areas that need improvement. Give him a brief outline of your new program, and explain to him the concept of the "pursuit of excellence." Discuss his personal, athletic, and academic goals and indicate areas in which you may be of help to him, letting him know that the most important thing you can offer him is that you care enough to try. Finally, ask his opinion of certain teammates and if he can recommend other athletes in the school or district who have not been in your football program. Before he leaves, schedule another brief meeting with him to discuss any items that you decide, in this interview, may require further attention. Use this person-to-person meeting to gain some insight into the player's character.

This period of evaluating and interviewing players should last about six weeks. However, during this time you should also be meeting casually with other faculty members and with coaches of other sports. You should begin promoting your program within the school family: Talk with students other than your players; find the student body leaders and soft-sell them on your program—not necessarily seeking their participation, but their support. Make your best effort during these six weeks to develop a strong rapport with as many on-campus people as possible— faculty, students, and administrators. The effort will pay strong dividends in the long run.

Develop Your Playbook

Meanwhile, back at home in the evenings you will be burning the midnight oil! You must develop the specifics of your offense, defense, and special teams. When you have completed your Xs and Os, compile all your offense into one playbook, your defense into another, and your kicking game into a third. Be sure the information is neat, concise, and easy to read. Reproduce a sufficient number of playbooks to allow all varsity players, varsity and lower division coaches, and the athletic director a complete set. Bind the playbooks in cardboard or vinyl binders, label and number each book, and set them aside until you are ready to release them.

The busiest time of your life will probably be the period between the time you are offered the position and the time your first six weeks on the job has ended. However, if the position is the right one and your positive energies are flowing, your excitement and adrenalin should bring you through it with relative ease. But in case you were thinking that the things covered in this chapter are all you need to accomplish during these six weeks, think again. All of the material in the following chapter and in the first half of chapter 6 must be completed during the same period of time. Keep smiling.

Chapter 5

Selling Your Program

Very few commodities, regardless of quality, sell themselves. Although the actual operation of your new football program must remain totally in your control, you are obliged by practical necessity to prevail upon others to make investments of time, emotions, and/or finances for somewhat intangible returns.

Legal arrangements can be made for most financial donations to be deducted as business expenses or charitable contributions. These are relatively easy sales compared to the difficult job of convincing others to invest countless hours of their time for purely subjective rewards like pride, a sense of accomplishment, or a feeling of being part of a winning effort. This, however, is your challenge as the leader of this winning effort. The more successful you are in this area, the easier it will be for you to accomplish your ultimate goal.

Pyramid Sales Concept

You will probably want to begin by researching the psychology of the "pyramid" sales concept, which is the most effective sales technique that I have ever encountered. It is a concept based upon two fundamental human instincts—the need to believe in something positive and the desire to succeed. The companies that have used this sales approach have masterfully created a marriage between two diametric spiritual concepts: the pure evangelist spirit and the sin of greed. The "pyramid" sales technique is one that is easy to adopt to your own needs once you have familiarized yourself with its basic approach. I suggest you sit in on some seminars sponsored by companies that employ this method of sales. Many such classes are conducted on a regular basis in cities and towns throughout the country. Try to visualize yourself conducting similar meetings with your staff. Create the "sales package" for your own program.

When you have absorbed this system and sales technique, construct your pyramid as shown in Figure 5.1.

Start Traditional Promotions

Be sure that you meet personally with the school administration to review your program. It is important that the administration know of any concerns, special projects, or progressive techniques that you may have in mind with regard to launching your program. Then set up a meeting with the conditioning coach, athletic director, and lower division head coach(es). Present your "sales package": the program, the "pursuit of excellence," academic and athletic achievement. Emphasize positive attitude and individual, team, and school benefits, as well as the potential rewards for everyone: better opportunities for coaches to advance, recognition of the athletic director for excellent administration, possible college scholarships for players, school pride, self-esteem, and general well-being. Send your disciples forth to spread the word. Assign them "sales territories," have them assign territories to their sales progeny, and so on. The word will spread and you can reinforce their efforts at every opportunity. Think of the potential! Think of the time and effort you can save for other important duties.

Once your pyramid system has had a chance to develop, you should start making arrangements to meet with parent and booster groups. It is most important to dispel quickly any wait-and-see attitudes they might have, and to present them with an exciting, positive image of you and the new program. Propose

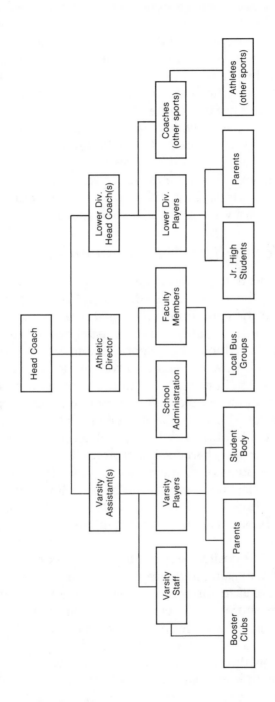

Figure 5.1. Sales pyramid for selling the new football program to your school, parents and community supporters.

some progressive ideas for their involvement in the program beyond the usual "get me some money" approach. Get these groups into the program, and they will volunteer ideas for fund-raising. Start some traditions—a booster club parade and pep rally the night before the opening game; a parent-booster supper the night before the homecoming game; senior parents' day before the last home game of the year. There is an endless number of bright, positive activities that can encourage these groups to participate in your dream, including fund-raising activities like Las Vegas Nights, old-timers' dances, and guest speaker programs. If you can create an atmosphere of enthusiasm among your adult supporters, they will help to elevate your program to heights beyond your grandest expectations.

Present Yourself to the Community

The simple fact that you have been hired as head football coach means that you have also necessarily been instated as a prominent person in the community. This is a rare opportunity that carries with it certain duties and responsibilities to the community as a whole. Much like celebrities and other prominent citizens, you will now be seen as a role model for young and old alike. Once you have accepted the position, you necessarily accept the trust of the people in the community. You must, therefore, present yourself to as many elements of the community as possible. Avail yourself of local retail services: shops, markets, cleaners, garages, barbers, liquor stores, and so forth. Utilize local businesses such as insurance agencies, automobile dealers, real estate agencies, restaurants, and banks. Meet with community business clubs like the Rotary Club and the Lyons Club. Make yourself known as the kind of gentleman the community can be proud of.

Take a bold and positive step toward gaining community support. Besides canvasing and supporting your local businesses, introduce yourself to the senior citizens in your area. Contact local retirement homes and nearby adult communities. Arrange to speak to senior citizen groups about the new football program at the high school. Perhaps you can devise a special program with the school administration to issue senior citizen passes for free admission to home games. It has been my experience that, although only a small percentage of people take advantage of the free admission, the senior citizens who do will number among your best and most faithful supporters. Those who attend your games enjoy being around younger people, and if they like the game of football, they usually become very loyal, very vocal fans. I have found that a gesture of consideration for the elderly is often as greatly appreciated by the rest of the community as it is by the senior citizens themselves.

Community support is more difficult to muster in some areas than it is in others. In isolated communities in rural America, and in the towns and small cities that have only one high school, it is relatively easy to create unanimity among the general population. But the larger cities and major metropolitan areas present altogether different problems. Densely populated areas often have several high schools, public and private, within the radius of a few miles. Each of these schools requires and requests both financial and volunteer support from the community at large. For this reason, as well as for basic ethical considerations, it is most important for you as head coach to present yourself as an integral part of your segment of this community. You must leave *your* mark in *your* territory in order to establish a solid base for community support.

Chapter 6

Organizing and Selecting a Staff

As you continue to burn the midnight oil during the first few weeks of your new job, you must now determine the size and makeup of your staff. Depending, of course, upon how many teams you plan to field within the program and the depth of player personnel at each level, you must plan to employ a coaching staff and a support staff of sufficient size to operate each division properly. Some high schools are large and so rich with talent that they may anticipate having enough athletes to field a completely separate offense, defense, and special unit in each division. Other schools have very few players and can barely maintain a small squad at the varsity level alone. Obviously, the staff requirements in each high school program will be different; however, the demands of most football programs will fall well within these parameters.

Develop a "Chain of Command"

The most effective way to analyze your staffing needs is to use the following "chain of command" chart as a basic guide, then tailor it to suit the requirements of your program (see Figure 6.1). From time to time programs are established using a co-head coach format. This format can be very advantageous in certain circumstances, particularly in large inner-city schools. A co-head coach system divides the share of the burden and allows each head coach to spend more time on the details of football execution. The major drawback of such a system, naturally, is the difficulty of matching two equally qualified personalities that complement each other so well and possess such mutual respect that they can function as one. Figure 6.2 shows a variation in the "chain of command" diagram to accommodate this format.

Find Candidates for Your Staff

As you can see from these diagrams, the larger programs may require as many as 25 coaches and almost that number of support staff. On the other hand, a friend of mine is currently head coach at a small high school in the state of Washington. He and two assistants (with some student managers) run a highly successful program. Everything is relative, and I am sure that situations similar to his exist in many high schools where community resources and qualified help are both extremely limited. However, there are often many untapped sources that high school head coaches overlook when attempting to recruit a staff. Naturally, budget plays a major role in building a staff, and most programs consolidate the coaching responsibilities on these charts to an even greater degree than budgets may demand. Nevertheless, do not hesitate to engage qualified or experienced volunteer coaches, if the opportunity arises.

During the organization process you must give strong consideration to the manner in which you will delegate responsibility and develop effective communication among staff members. Your own "chain of command" chart, drafted by you and designed to meet your specific needs, will form the basis for this important part of your staff organization. I suggest that you first determine the kinds of responsibilities that you feel should be delegated, and then, referring to the chart, select the staff positions most suited to taking on these responsibilities. For instance, the responsibility for the physical health and therapeutic care of your athletes should be delegated to the team doctor and head athletic trainer; the team manager should be given the responsibility

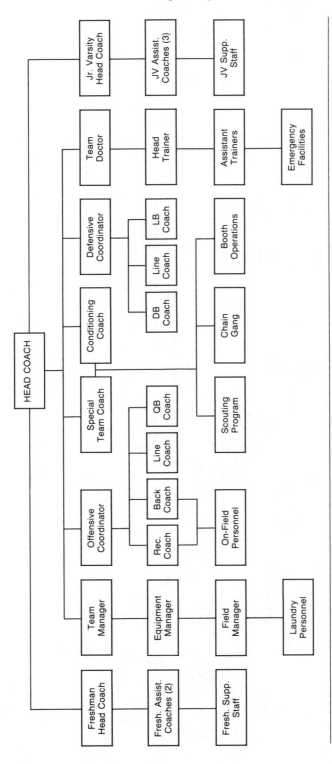

Figure 6.1. Chain of command for coaching and support staff (single head coach format).

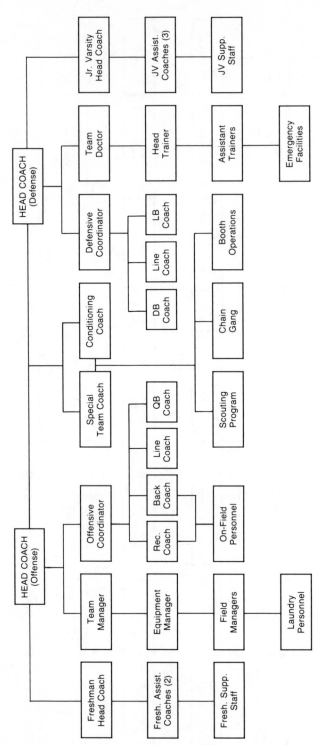

Figure 6.2. Chain of command for coaching and support staff (co-head coach format).

of having all necessary equipment, gear, material, and supplies properly functioning and available for use as required; the defensive coordinator should be solely responsible for developing a preliminary defensive game plan each week from scouting input; and so on through the first line of staff positions below the head coach on your "chain of command" chart.

Although your chart will indicate the kinds of duties for which each of your assistants will be responsible, the amount of responsibility you wish to delegate will be entirely up to you. The chances are that this decision will be based on the assistant that you select to fill a particular position and how you feel about that person's ability to handle responsibility. An individual's ability to handle authority must also be a major factor in deciding the amount of responsibility you will delegate. Be sure that you understand the degree of authority that must accompany each responsibility. Of course, ultimate responsibility and authority rest with the head coach, but delegated responsibility must be accompanied by corresponding delegated authority.

Your "chain of command" chart will also indicate the line of communication that should develop within your program. Although as head coach your door should always be open to any staff member with pressing problems, the general line of communication to and from the head coach should relay through the first-line assistants. This process should not be used to isolate you from the extremities of your staff, but rather to allow your first-line assistants to establish their own leadership credibility aided by your highly visible confidence in their ability to exercise that leadership and the responsibility you have given them. This strong expression of confidence in your staff will only increase your own credibility as a self-confident leader, which will result in open and effective communication throughout the program.

You will now need to think about choosing your assistant coaches. Almost any head coach will first contact potential assistants with whom he has had some past association and for whom he has respect; everyone feels most comfortable having proven and reliable people in key positions. The next most logical area to investigate for potential assistant coaches would be within the high school faculty itself. Coaches in other sports, or those from the preceding program, may be capable assistants. Teachers are often qualified and experienced football coaches who may fit into your program in some capacity. However, the people who are most frequently overlooked are youth football coaches and parents. It seems that some high school head coaches become a bit arrogant and snobbish when it comes to considering youth football coaches or players' fathers as possible assistant coaches. With no knowledge of such individuals' background or experience, these parochial thinkers tend to prejudge the qualifications of those they consider to be "outsiders." The fact is that some of the best coaches I have ever known have been or still are involved in youth football. Of course, all youth football coaches are not highly qualified, but unfortunately, neither are all coaches at any level. However, one virtue that makes accomplished youth football coaches immediate assets to a high school program is their love for, and ability to communicate with, young people.

Every so often, a father who happens to be highly qualified as a football coach due to his extensive playing experience, or even due to a significant coaching background, will volunteer his coaching services. More likely you will get volunteer offers from far less qualified, but equally well-meaning fathers. The father-son relationship can be quite delicate and often may detract from both the credibility of the parent/coach and the performance of the athlete. It is advisable in these circumstances to separate the father's and son's activities as much as possible. For instance, a well-qualified parent/coach can function very effectively in a different division from his son, or coaching a different position than his son plays. A closer working relationship than that is not recommended, and the situation demands thorough scrutiny whenever father and son function at the same level of participation.

You must examine all offers carefully; do not reject any of them out-of-hand. Although a man may not be sufficiently qualified as an assistant coach in any division, he will undoubtedly have some assets or background that qualifies him to help your program in other areas. He may be a doctor, a physical therapist, or a certified athletic trainer. He may work in the computer field or in sporting goods. Even if his occupation is not directly related to your needs, his willingness to help the program is sufficient reason alone to consider using him for such support jobs as film or video camera operator, spotter, scouting assistant, equipment handler or even as a member of the "chain gang."

The more positions you can fill with willing, responsible people, the more time you will have to concentrate on football execution.

Additional coaching assistants, particularly for the lower division teams, may be recruited from the ranks of the more recently graduated football players from your school. They must, of course, still live in the community, and must be able to fit the time comfortably into their current college or work schedules. These young men often make excellent freshman or junior varsity assistant coaches, specializing in the positions they have recently played at your school.

Select Your Assistant Coaches

As you interview potential assistant coaches, be sure to keep extensive notes on their qualifications and the personal impressions that they leave with you. You must analyze and collate all of this data to decide on the most cohesive and productive staff possible, overall and at each division. Weigh and balance each candidate's background, experience, youth, maturity, attitude, personality, and past performance so that you can properly align compatible personalities in positions that demand contiguity.

Your initial priority in the selection process should focus on the first-line assistant coaches. Finding the most qualified lower division head coaches available is of paramount importance. These must be special people who have both the patience and the charisma to teach young athletes sound fundamental football and at the same time instill in them a love for, and a strong desire to play, the game of football. The proper selection of lower division head coaches will insure a solid foundation for success in your football program for years to come. Since you have already selected and hired a conditioning coach, you should now determine if he will also be able to function in any other first-line capacity. Once that has been decided, you can begin making selections from candidates for your first-line assistant coaching positions in the following order: (1) offensive coordinator, (2) defensive coordinator, and (3) special teams coordinator.

When all of the first-line assistant coaches and lower division head coaches have been selected you should give them the names and background information of other coaches who are qualified to be position coaches or general assistants. At that point, your coordinators and lower division head coaches must conduct their own interviews. They should then present their recommendations to you, and finally, you must reject, adjust, or approve these recommendations to complete the balance of your coaching staff.

Recruit Student Support Staff

Your next priority is to recruit students for the noncoaching positions that are necessary to operate an efficient program. These positions must be filled by students who are not football players and should be given to the most qualified people, regardless of sex. You may find, as I have, that handicapped youngsters often develop into reliable aides. The positions that should be filled at the student level are:

- *Team Manager*—a student who enjoys football and is intelligent and well respected by his or her peers; a reliable and responsible senior in general good health. The team manager is responsible for coordinating all student support staff activities and for having all necessary equipment, gear, material, and supplies properly functioning and available for coaches and players when required.
- *Assistant Managers*—one varsity assistant, and one assistant for each lower division team. The qualifications for assistant managers are similar to those for team manager. The varsity assistant should be a junior, the junior varsity assistant a sophomore, and the freshman team assistant a ninth grader. All assistants are under the direction of the team manager, and, in order to maintain continuity and a certain degree of pride in achievement, the assistants should be promoted to team manager as they become seniors.
- *Equipment Manager*—a student who enjoys football and is intelligent and well respected by his or her peers; a reliable, organized senior with a high mechanical aptitude and good administrative skills. The equipment manager is under the direction of the team manager, and is responsible for the proper working condition, repair, and replacement of all gear and equipment used by coaches and players.
- *Assistant Equipment Managers*—one assistant (a junior and sophomore) for each lower division team. The qualifications for these positions are similar to those for equipment

manager. The assistant equipment managers should be promoted to equipment manager as they become seniors.

- *Field Manager*—a senior who enjoys football, is hard-working, intelligent, reliable, and responsible, and who enjoys working outdoors. The field manager works closely with the groundskeeper and team manager to prepare stadium facilities for home games; he or she also surveys and reports on visiting team facilities for away games. The field manager is responsible for the condition, repair, and/or replacement of booth equipment, field phones, and sideline equipment such as benches, tables, and water fountains, and also prepares sidelines for games per the instructions of the head coach and the team manager.

- *Laundry and Uniform Care Personnel*—two seniors. These are the only paid student positions. Sufficient funds for this operation should be obtained through fundraisers. These students should be selected from the student/work program based on ability first and need second. The positions involve everyday operation of laundry for towels, socks, and underwear of players; one day per week laundering of game uniforms; one day per week laundering of practice uniforms; and occasional game uniform repairs.

- *Student Trainers and Tapers*—as many as the head trainer requires, and determines to be qualified, to handle taping and minor first-aid under his or her direct supervision.

- *Spotters, Stats, and "Key Factors" Personnel*—between three and five students, preferably seniors or juniors, to function as booth and on-field spotters, and play-by-play stat keepers. One student to maintain "key factors" (time-outs left for each team, time left on clock, key injuries, catastrophe procedures, etc.).

An additional noncoaching position that may be filled by either a student, teacher, or parent is that of computerized scouting specialist. Locate a qualified computer programmer and recruit him or her into setting up and maintaining a regular computerized scouting analysis system for your use during the season.

Select a Medical Team

Finally, as director of the entire football program, you must be concerned with the health and well-being of all players at all levels of the program. The selection of the most qualified doctors and athletic trainers available is a very important responsibility. It is possible that an excellent G.P. or internist may not be properly qualified in sports medicine. As a general rule, doctors who specialize in emergency medicine and orthopedics seem to have the best understanding of sports injuries. Ask your school administrators and school nurse for information about local physicians and surgeons. In your search for the team physician, keep in mind that he or she must be available or on call during all practices and must be able to attend every game, whether at home or away.

Unless the school already has a certified trainer on staff, you should solicit recommendations for a head trainer from your team doctor. The head trainer must be a *certified* athletic trainer and available to attend all games, practices, and after-game injury clinics. He or she will be responsible for recruiting, selecting, and training assistants based on the budget and available volunteers. The head trainer also has the job of arranging for hospital and emergency facilities, including paramedic ambulances for home games, and of maintaining a proper training/therapy facility on campus.

Meet With Your Staff

Once your decisions are made and your final selections are complete, put each staff member's name in its proper place on the chain of command chart. Begin scheduling individual meetings with them all to discuss their positions thoroughly, including their duties and responsibilities, the people they will be working with, and if applicable, the people they will be subordinate to. Also outline any off-season or extra assignments you would like them to handle. Give all staff members the opportunity in these interviews to candidly discuss any problems or apprehensions they might have with their positions or circumstances. Make sure they fully understand why you have selected them for this particular position.

After these individual meetings, schedule a meeting to include the entire staff. At this meeting there should be a large chain of command chart on either a blackboard or a poster board with the name of each staff member located in its proper position. Individual 8 1/2″ × 11″ copies of this chart should be distributed to the group. Review this chart thoroughly, making sure that each staff member understands his or her position in the chain and how the chain works to the benefit of the program. You should use this meeting to announce your selection of a top-line assistant coach who will function as ''assistant head coach'' and will automatically become interim head coach in your absence due to illness, injury, or other emergencies. Your players, coaches, and staff should understand and accept this fact, and it is your job to be sure that the assistant head coach is well qualified and always adequately informed so that he may properly perform his duties as interim head coach. You must convince everyone, including the athletic director and school administration, of your faith in his ability to handle the responsibility if required.

The only other item of business at this meeting will be to distribute and review a schedule of future staff meetings to be held in the off-season, including projected topics of discussion. Instruct your entire staff to be fully prepared for these meetings so that you can cover the agenda in the shortest possible time. How well each staff member prepares for these meetings will help you determine how well each handles responsibility, and thus how to make future decisions delegating duties and authority.

You should finish all of the work up to this point no later than March 15 if you wish to set up a full-scale off-season program.

Chapter 7

Recruiting Athletes

Immediate Recruiting

The qualified and prepared head coach can develop the atmosphere necessary for a successful football program. Creating a positive winning attitude, a well-planned, effective organization, and a unique, innovative system of play is well within his power. But to be a consistent champion, you need athletes! Striving to be a consistent champion is a fitting long-range goal in the "pursuit of excellence," and bringing as many good athletes into your program as possible will afford you the wherewithal to do this. You must *recruit* the athletes—once you have done that, the great challenge of pursuing excellence is yours alone to meet.

A successful recruiting program can be approached in much the same way as goal planning, discussed in chapter 1. The process is divided into four categories: immediate recruiting, short-term recruiting, near-future recruiting, and long-term recruiting. As in goal planning, you should approach these categories in consecutive order so that you can build a solid foundation for future recruiting efforts. Recruiting athletes for your immediate needs begins with securing returning players at all levels of participation in your program. The best way to accomplish this is by personal contact with each player. You can motivate these athletes to return to your program with a new enthusiasm by stimulating their interest in the newness of your program, by being a positive role model on campus, and by encouraging them to pursue excellence in academics as well as athletics. Recruiting returning athletes is the most crucial step in your overall recruiting effort, and unless you are successful in this area, any further recruiting will be severely hindered. You will need to be patient and spend as much time and effort as necessary to successfully accomplish this first recruiting goal.

Short-Term Recruiting

The successful completion of this stage of recruiting will give a strong boost to your short-term recruiting efforts, that is, to the recruiting of on-campus athletes who have not yet decided to play football. Once the word gets around campus that you care about your players; that you plan to develop an exciting new program designed to instill pride in the team, the school, and the community; that the players themselves believe in your ability to help them accomplish positive athletic, personal, and academic goals, the groundwork will be laid for you to make contact with these other athletes.

In order to avoid conflicts with other coaches on campus while recruiting for your short-term needs, you will need to exercise a great deal of tact. Many of the highly successful coaches that I have interviewed recommend a series of procedures specifically aimed at encouraging cooperation among school coaches. These procedures include:

- Encouraging your players to play two sports in addition to football (basketball or wrestling in the winter—baseball, track, or soccer in the spring).
- Prevailing upon the athletic director to establish a general policy requesting all coaches in boys' sports to encourage their athletes to play at least one other sport.

- Meeting with coaches of other sports in your school to discuss individual athletes and how participation in more than one sport will enhance each athlete's ability.
- Presenting a plan to the coaches and athletic director for a "gentlemen's agreement" among all coaches not to recruit athletes from sports played during the same season. If a young athlete wishes to change activities in such circumstances, the coach receiving the new player must ask the young man to first discuss the change thoroughly with the athletic director, who should then help him to decide on a course of action that is in his best interest.

These procedures, although aimed at encouraging cooperation among coaches who are recruiting, will also work in the best interests of the athletes and the overall athletic program.

Near-Future Recruiting

Recruiting for your near-future needs involves recruiting off-campus talent. Your own enthusiastic returning players will once again play an important part in this quest. They will undoubtedly know the names and locations of most of the best athletes in your area, as they have probably played with them in youth sports. They may even initiate contact with those off-campus athletes whom they know well. Before recruiting off-campus talent, though, be sure to familiarize yourself with all state, county, city, conference, and district rules and limitations that govern this type of recruiting. Be sure you understand all rules for transfers and district residence requirements. Remember that a championship season can be ruined, a school reputation can be flawed, and a coach's career—yours—can be damaged by illegal, immoral, or unethical recruiting practices. Recruit vigorously, but ethically.

When legally recruiting athletes within your jurisdiction there are two things that you should never do: (1) criticize the coach of another school, and (2) recruit a varsity player from another program. A basic sense of ethics and fair play should demand your attention to these two rules. If you break these rules, your reputation as a coach will be in jeopardy. Meet with all of your varsity assistant and lower division coaches to discuss all of these recruiting rules and regulations. Be certain that they fully understand the manner in which you wish off-campus recruiting to be conducted. Their primary function when scouting should be to obtain available talent legitimately and to make recommendations for final recruiting.

Long-Term Recruiting

The best, and ultimately the most beneficial, type of recruiting is long-term recruiting. This final stage of recruiting involves concentrating on the junior high school and youth football athletes and coaches, which will take much of your personal time and patience, and a great deal of school cooperation, to be truly effective. Most young athletes up to age 14 are greatly influenced by their coaches, and so a massive public relations effort aimed at the junior high school and youth football coaches is necessary. There are a number of such public relations activities usually considered legitimate if properly conducted and administered, including personal visits to practices, coaching clinics hosted by your school, off-season youth football camps held on your campus, limited offers of your school athletic facilities, recruiting rallies, and so on. Be as genuinely helpful to these coaches and programs as you can be. Donate equipment and supplies to them whenever possible; take out ads in their game program; convince the school to allow them to practice on the soccer field or baseball outfield if they have no permanent practice facility of their own. Arrange to have playoff or championship games in your stadium or playing field. Most of these junior high school and youth football programs function on a very limited budget, and any assistance you can offer will be greatly appreciated. Your efforts will help create a positive image of your program and your school to everyone.

To aid in these annual recruiting drives, you might consider enlisting the help of certain student groups. Student artists can develop posters and flyers advertising recruiting rallies and special events. Student musicians, singers, and entertainers can help plan unique, youth-oriented entertainment for rallies and parties. The more students you can involve in the recruiting process, the more enjoyable this process will become for the school and the more successful it will be. It can be yet another way to instill enthusiasm and pride in your new program.

Finally, make doubly sure that everything is legal and above-board. Be sure to clear all plans for special recruiting activities with the school administration and athletic director. Invite anyone to these activities that you feel will help the recruiting effort—recent alumni, the booster club president, coaches of other sports, parents. Try to plan at least two special recruiting events during the spring semester of each year.

Chapter 8

Beginning the Off-Season Program

I can imagine most of you right now are looking skyward and asking, "Is this guy crazy, or what? Do I have to go through all this just to be a head football coach? When do we get to the football?" The answers to these questions, in order, are:

1. I do not believe that I am certifiable; however, on the subject of poor high school football coaching I do have a tendency toward limited tolerance. In fact, unprepared or inadequate high school head coaches drive me nuts! I hope you will understand my zeal to eliminate irresponsible behavior from this profession. If, at times, what you have read has seemed a bit "preachy" or overbearing, please accredit that to my passion for excellence at all levels of the great sport of football.

2. No, of course you do not have to go through all this just to be a head football coach. However, if you truly care about the sport, the young people you are developing, and your own self-worth, you will probably decide that you want to strive for excellence. This book is simply a guide to help you pursue that goal.

3. The preceding seven chapters were written to help you prepare for and assume command of a high school football program, to deal properly with the role of leader, and to increase your awareness of the major duties and responsibilities of a high school head coach. The following seven chapters will concentrate on the specific structure and activities of an actual football program, from off-season to postseason.

Most off-season football programs at the high school level are ordinary, boring drudgery—weight lifting, running, and exercise. This type of off-season program chases away new recruits faster than a pride of lions chases away a herd of zebra. It creates an impression that football is all work and no fun. We, as coaches, know that hard work is essential to success, but young people must be guided into a *desire* for hard work. The most effective way to accomplish this is to create enthusiasm for the game itself and develop an off-season conditioning program that makes the work as enjoyable as possible—one that uses competitive and recreational techniques to develop strength, quickness, speed, and stamina.

This chapter outlines a compulsory ten-week in-school spring program with an optional six-week summer vacation maintenance program. The basic strength and stretching program started at the beginning of the spring semester by your conditioning coach (see chapter 4) will lead directly into this full-scale off-season program.

Many schools throughout the country provide the last class period of the day an an optional physical education or study hall period. If your school has this policy, you could use this time for your off-season conditioning period in the spring semester and for prepractice and meetings in the fall semester. All varsity football players should be required to take this class, provided it does not conflict with a required subject. If you do not have the last-period option, your off-season program should take place immediately after school. In any case, individual classes or sessions should not exceed one hour in length to eliminate the possibilities of boredom, overwork, or fatigue. Young people tend to begin losing their concentration and attentiveness in classes that exceed one hour, and it is always better to leave a group wanting more, than to leave a group fast asleep.

Counting backwards ten weeks from the last full week before final examinations will give you the starting date for the off-season program (allow additional time for school holidays and vacations as necessary). In most cases this date will be somewhere around April 1st. The following program is similar to those that have produced highly successful results for many people, including several of my colleagues and myself.

In-School Spring Program

Week number one of the spring conditioning period should emphasize an orientation to your new program and the beginning of an eight-part series on "Teaching the Game." The first session should consist of general introductions of staff and players, an outline of the off-season program, and a brief description of your coaching philosophy, including your feelings about discipline, hard work, honesty, desire, and dedication. A short question-and-answer period with direct, honest responses to questions (liberally laced with humor) always tends to start things off with a good, positive, open feeling of interaction among your staff, the players, and yourself.

Two sessions of "Teaching the Game" should be included in this first week. For the first session, put together an amusing and informative presentation on the history of football from its inception to the present day. Use stories, anecdotes, and audio and videotapes with the most entertainment potential to communicate the idea that the game of football can be fun to play and that it has a rich tradition of which one can be proud to be a part. The second session should begin a three-part series dealing with rules, the first part to include the distribution of rule books for home study, discussion of why it is important to know the rules, and an explanation of basic concepts.

The rest of the week should include a transition from the conditioning program, which was instituted at the beginning of the semester, into a competitive weight lifting program extending through the balance of the off-season. Week number one of the off-season program would be scheduled as shown in Table 8.1.

Week number two should emphasize the start of a competitive weight lifting program to be supervised by your conditioning coach and a continuation of the "Teaching the Game" series on rules. Using the progress chart (Table 8.2) with maximum lifts indicated for each player as a starting point, develop the competitive weight lifting program as a contest between athletes in

Table 8.1 Off-Season Program

Week No. _____One_____ Starting On _____30 March 1987_____

Day	Activity	Emphasis
Monday	ORIENTATION CLASS with entire staff and all Varsity players	General introductions; outline program; discuss philosophy; questions and answers
Tuesday	Session #1 "Teaching the Game"	Presentation on history of football; stories, anecdotes and videotapes
Wednesday	Stretching and weight lifting	Continuation of program started at beginning of semester; work for maximum power lifts
Thursday	Session #2 "Teaching the Game"	Part one of series on rules; basic concepts; issue rule books for study
Friday	Stretching and weight lifting	Maximum bench, squat, military and clean for first entry on progress chart*

*NOTES: *Progress Chart* should be drafted to show individual weekly personal achievement and strength development similar to sample in Table 8.2

the same weight categories. The object of the contest is either to lift more weight than the others in one's category, or to make more progress in weight lifting than the others in that category. This allows each athlete two ways to succeed—competing against each other and competing against oneself. At the end of the off-season conditioning period the final results will be listed on the chart and the winners announced. Prizes should be awarded to all the winners (T-shirts or sweat-shirts appropriately imprinted). The first-prize winner might receive an engraved nameplate on a permanent trophy to be kept in the football trophy case.

The "Teaching the Game" series dealing with rules should now concentrate on the understanding of specific rules and penalties, concluding with a question-and-answer session to be conducted by a league game official. The final sessions should

Table 8.2 Weight Lifting Progress Chart

NAME OF PLAYER

Category By Player's Weight	Adams, D.	Alberts, R.	Alberts, W.	Anno, S.	Bixby, W.	Bonnet, M.	Brown, M.	Burelson, R.	Cacciatore, W.	Cain, D.	Cassell, M.	Coleman, T.	Connors, J.	Daley, W.	Danby, E.	Davis, K.	Davis, Sam	Davis, Steve	Dennehy, B.	Enderle, F.	Evans, D.	George, J.
	C	A	B	D	D	D	B	D	C	A	C	C	C	A	B	C	B	A	C	C	C	
BENCH - start																						
- week 5																						
- week 9																						
SQUAT - start																						
- week 5																						
- week 9																						
MILITARY - start																						
- week 5																						
- week 9																						
CLEAN - start																						
- week 5																						
- week 9																						
Category Winner																						

Weight Categories: A = 230 lbs. and over; B = 200 lbs. to 230 lbs.; C = 170 lbs. to 200 lbs.; D = under 170 lbs.

cover both the rule book and officiating in general. Week number two of the off-season program, then, would be scheduled as shown in Table 8.3.

The competitive weight lifting program should continue through week number three. "Teaching the Game" now begins a four-part series on great teams and great players. Prepare each part of this series by combining stories, films, and videocassettes (produced by the NCAA, NFL, etc.). This same format would be repeated through week number four (see Table 8.4).

Week number five will be the half-way point of your off-season program. During this week the conditioning program shifts into high gear with the addition of an aerobics class. A specialized nondance aerobics exercise program for young athletes should have been developed earlier in the off-season by one of the varsity assistant coaches. The best approach for researching and developing such a program would be to enroll this assistant in a local aerobics class shortly after he has been hired so that he can learn proper instructing techniques and valuable routines to be used in developing health, stamina, flexibility, and quickness. He will then be able to plan and teach the aerobics phase of your

Table 8.3 Off-Season Program

Week No. _____Two_____ **Starting On** _____6 April 1987_____

Day	Activity	Emphasis
Monday	Stretching and weight lifting	Begin competitive weight lifting program conducted by conditioning coach
Tuesday	Session #3 "Teaching the Game"	Discuss rule book; specific rules and penalties
Wednesday	Stretching and weight lifting	Continue competitive program
Thursday	Session #4 "Teaching the Game"	League game official to conduct question and answer session
Friday	Stretching and weight lifting	Continue competitive program

Table 8.4   Off-Season Program

Week No. ___Three/Four___ **Starting On** _____**13 April 1987**_____

Monday	Stretching and weight lifting	Continue competitive program
Tuesday	"Teaching the Game"	Great teams and great players series
Wednesday	Stretching and weight lifting	Continue competitive program
Thursday	"Teaching the Game"	Great teams and great players series
Friday	Stretching and weight lifting	Continue competitive program

off-season program. In the meantime, the competitive stretching and weight lifting program should continue. On Friday of week number five all your varsity players can be tested for maximum bench, squat, military, and clean. The results of these maximum lifts should be entered on the halfway column on the progress chart (see Table 8.2). This procedure should be repeated at the end of week number nine.

This same weekly format should be repeated through week number nine with all work in weight lifting and aerobics intensifying each week (see Table 8.5).

Spring Conditioning Wrap-Up

Week number ten will wind up the off-season conditioning program with a series of fun events aimed at sustaining a positive image of your program throughout the summer hiatus. A three-day Intra-Squad Olympics, an Intra-Squad Touch Football Game, and an award presentation at a team picnic are the high points of the off-season program.

The Intra-Squad Olympics is a friendly competition between four teams which include all of your varsity players. These teams should be selected and supervised by you and your staff in order to maintain a fair and equitable competitive balance. The events would include sprints and medium distance races, individual

Table 8.5 Off-Season Program

Week No. ___Five-Nine___ **Starting On** _____27 April 1987_____

Day	Activity	Emphasis
Monday	Stretching and weight lifting	Continue competitive program
Tuesday	Aerobics exercise program	Non-dance intense exercises designed to develop cardio-vascular and respiratory stamina and body flexibility
Wednesday	Stretching and weight lifting	Continue competitive program
Thursday	Aerobics exercise program	Continue program under supervision of assistant coach
Friday	Stretching and weight lifting	Continue competitive program*

*NOTES: On Friday of the fifth and ninth weeks only, all athletes will be tested for maximum lifts and progress shall be entered on the chart.

strength events, relay races of various types, jumping competitions, and a variety of light, recreational activities such as obstacle races, sack races, tug-of-war, and so on. Each event should be assigned point values for first, second, and third place, and the team having the most points at the end of the three-day competition will be declared the winner.

The varsity football team can be divided into two relatively equal teams to play the Intra-Squad Touch Football Game. This game will be basically a passing game with mock blocking and line play. It should be conducted as a regular game (scoring and time to be kept on the scoreboard), with two regular league officials working the game and a coaching staff assigned to each sideline to control substitutions and play calling.

The final day of your off-season program will be Friday of this tenth week. If weather permits, the festivities should be held outdoors. If not, they should be held in the gymnasium or cafeteria. I suggest that you start with a guest speaker, preferably a prominent football personality (either active or retired) who has also distinguished himself academically or professionally. Your guest, unless he is a nationally known figure, should have something that distinguishes him locally to give him immediate name recognition in your community. The speaker's topic can be on any area of sport, but it should be motivational in nature rather than instructional, and also should strongly support the basic concept of the "pursuit of excellence." Following the guest speaker should be an awards presentation. Various types of awards should be given for a wide variety of activities: awards for the winners of the competitive weight lifting program; awards to the winning team of the Intra-Squad Olympics; a trophy for the winning Intra-Squad Touch Football Team; special awards for outstanding self-discipline and team leadership; special certificates for the season's captains, who are to be selected by you and your coaching staff with input from the players.

The program might conclude with an early picnic supper for the players, staff, athletic director, and school administrators. Although the competitive events earlier in the week can be widely publicized and open to the general student population, the last day should be confined exclusively to the football family. This will help foster pride in being part of an exclusive group, while at the same time make many of those who cannot attend feel that being a football player is indeed something special.

In addition to this off-season conditioning program, you may have, by conference or league rules, a spring practice period. You may also choose to participate in passing leagues or tournaments during the spring and summer. Preparation for these additional activities must not preempt the conditioning program. These extra events are often quite important to the proper development of a good program, but they must be approached as a separate entity—an extracurricular activity to the extracurricular activity, if you will. They must have a holistic life of their own, apart from the basic off-season program, so that your off-season conditioning program will not be compromised and will maintain its proper status in your football program.

You, as head coach, must oversee the entire off-season program even though you will be conducting only a portion of the program yourself. However, there are other preseason activities besides the conditioning program that will require your more direct involvement. These activities, which will be dealt with in detail in the next chapter, include:

— Developing a list of priorities and a detailed practice schedule for preseason.
— Meeting with school officials to inform them of your summer program and preseason plans; obtaining all permits and authorizations.
— Working with quarterbacks, running backs, and receivers on technique and timing.
— Assigning staff to specific responsibilities of organizing, repairing, and/or replacing all football and safety equipment and supplies.
— Working closely with the parent or teacher in charge of the computerized scouting system to develop the precise program you desire for the season.

Using this approach to an off-season conditioning program will accomplish all of the basic goals of any off-season program— developing strength, quickness, speed, and stamina—and will result in major dividends for you, your staff, the players, and the football program itself.

The orientation class, held on the first day, can be designed to create the first positive image of your new program and yourself as head coach. The eight-part series on "Teaching the Game" will give the class a worthwhile educational experience, helping your players to understand and appreciate the game of football, as well as attracting marginal athletes to the program who previously had reservations about playing football.

The friendly rivalry of the competitive weight lifting program will foster the development of self-discipline as well as a desire to win. The music in aerobics and the exercise done in unison will create an attitude of togetherness and will undoubtedly be the most fun any group of young football players has ever had, while at the same time getting cardiovascular systems, legs, and respiratory systems into peak condition. Aerobics will also develop stamina more effectively than most other forms of exercise.

Finally, the Intra-Squad Olympics and Intra-Squad Touch-Football Game will foster the competitive spirit and winning attitude developed in the weight lifting program and will promote a feeling of camaraderie among the players. These events are aimed particularly at helping the players and coaches establish an informal relationship to encourage open communication. These concluding events in your spring off-season program afford your coaching staff an excellent opportunity to evaluate the players' athletic ability, emotional structure, and leadership qualities prior to preparing for the season.

Optional Summer Program

The award presentations, guest speaker, and picnic emphasize team pride, desire, and dedication which will keep the players' interest and enthusiasm primed through the summer vacation. It may even stimulate a few additional volunteers to participate in your summer conditioning program (see Table 8.6 for sample schedule). This program should be supervised by both you and your conditioning coach, and if possible, be conducted in school facilities. If the facilities are not available, arrangements must be made for the use of municipal or private facilities.

Table 8.6 Optional Summer Program

Week No. ___One-Six___ **Starting On** ___6 July 1987___

Day	Activity	Emphasis
Monday	Weight lifting and agility	Upper body weight program on circuits; rope jumping, footwork drills
Tuesday	Weight lifting and agility	Lower body and leg weight program on circuits; swimming
Wednesday	Weight lifting and agility	Upper body weight program on circuits; rope jumping, footwork drills
Thursday	Weight lifting and agility	Lower body and leg weight program on circuits; swimming
Friday	OFF	

Although the program is called "optional," it should be considered mandatory for players who do not have employment or pressing family conflicts over the six weeks that it is conducted. The summer program is an excellent way to maintain the conditioning achieved during the spring program.

Chapter 9

Preparing for the Season

Preparation for the season can be divided into three major time periods: (1) spring off-season planning and practice, (2) summer development and practice, and (3) fall preseason evaluation and practice. The spring planning period is, by far, the most demanding of your time. That is why I have recommended in the previous chapters that you delegate the responsibility of conducting most of the off-season conditioning program to your assistant coaches.

Off-Season Planning and Practice

While the players and several of your assistant coaches are deeply immersed in the off-season conditioning program, you, your offensive coordinator, and your defensive coordinator will start to formulate the details for spring, summer, and fall practice priorities. The first step is to evaluate the playbooks that you have previously developed relative to the player talent you will have (see chapter 4). Using the player information that you compiled at the beginning of the semester, together with observations of off-season progress, you should be able to project a fairly accurate forecast of the talent you will have at the beginning of the preseason. With the playbooks as a guide, you and the coordinators should reanalyze the talent of each athlete in terms of the physical demands of the positions they will be most suited to play. The best available athletes should then be fitted into their proper positions to whatever depth your numbers allow. Once you have done this, you will have a relatively clear picture of what you can achieve as a team offensively and defensively, and what you cannot achieve.

With this evaluation you can begin to organize a list of priorities that you wish to accomplish in the summer and preseason. This list of priorities should be designed as a source of information for you and your staff concerning your players' range of ability and their potential for progress within the context of the offense and defense that you have outlined. For example: What kind of a passing game can you expect to develop? Do you have the size and strength to develop an inside power running game? Proper spring planning and scheduling will help to answer all of the questions that you may have regarding the potential performance of your team. If your spring organization and planning are meticulous, you should be able to arrive at satisfactory answers in the relatively short time that will be available in the summer and preseason. You should organize minute-by-minute practice schedules, and establish major criteria for judging progress and potential well in advance. The practice schedules should be quite specific regarding the mechanics that are to be worked on at any given time. In this way it is possible to properly measure and analyze both individual and team progress. The scheduling of preseason practices will vary from school to school for many reasons. First, league rules regulating the starting date, conditioning period, practice hours, and allowable contact will determine approach and timing. Second, the size and makeup of your program (number of teams, number of players, size of staff, etc.) will determine just how much can be accomplished within a given period of time. Finally, the nature and availability of your practice facilities may have an influence on the length of time you can practice. All these factors must be considered during the spring planning period prior to drafting your spring, summer, and preseason practice schedules, thus eliminating delays and confusion at the beginning of each practice period and creating player confidence in you and your staff.

Once the priorities have been established and the details of scheduling worked out, assign your defensive coordinator the task of drafting both the finished priorities list and the final practice schedules for the spring, summer, and fall. He should be responsible for having everything neatly typed and enough copies made for the entire staff (all divisions), the athletic director, the school nurse, the school administration office, the team doctor(s), and the head trainer. Copies of the spring and summer practice schedules should also be posted on all team bulletin boards.

Meanwhile, you and your offensive coordinator should begin late-spring informal workouts with all quarterbacks, running backs, and receivers. These workouts can be held at almost any time—lunch period, before school, after school, weekends—whatever is most practical and convenient. They need not be more than 30-minute sessions and should concentrate solely on the mechanics of the passing game. The following elements of the passing game that are most critical, and frequently improperly coached, should be introduced to these positions prior to the summer vacation:

- *Quarterbacks:* footwork, throwing mechanics, reading coverage keys, knowledge of the "passing tree" and how each receiver runs the patterns in that tree
- *Running backs:* footwork, blocking keys, catching mechanics, knowledge of the "passing tree" and running precise patterns
- *Receivers:* footwork, catching mechanics, reading coverage keys, knowledge of the "passing tree" and running precise patterns

If you and/or your offensive coordinator are not totally familiar with the proper mechanics required by all of these positions within the passing game, please research it thoroughly *before* you teach your players. With all the books and magazine articles that have been written by unquestioned masters on the mechanics of the passing game—from Sid Gillman to Bill Walsh to La-Vell Edwards—there is bound to be a style that is compatible with your offense. By the end of the spring semester, your "touch" positions should be sufficiently schooled in these proper mechanics to allow them to practice on their own during summer vacation. When preseason practice begins, it will be apparent which players worked the hardest over the summer, not only because of their technical advantage over the others, but also because of their increased self-confidence, obvious self-discipline, and burgeoning ability to lead.

Prior to final exam week of the spring semester, you should schedule three very important meetings—one with your coaching staff, one with your support staff, and one with the school officials (athletic director, principal, and dean of athletics). Prepare a specific agenda for each meeting. Be thorough but concise—keep the meetings as brief as possible.

The following is a list of important items to be included on the agenda for Meeting #1 with your entire coaching staff:

1. Review priorities list.
2. Review summer and preseason practice schedules.
3. Issue playbooks and discuss imperative coaching points relating to technique, mechanics, or general execution.
4. Introduce the concept of *preparing for catastrophe* which will be further developed during regular preseason coaching meetings.

"Catastrophe" can be anything from a critical penalty to losing your star player with an injury on the first play of the game. Catastrophe generally causes confusion; people often panic and lose confidence in their ability to cope with the unexpected disaster. In order to cope with disaster, you must first eliminate the confusion. This is the goal of "preparing for catastrophe," a program based on two ideas with which your staff should be thoroughly indoctrinated: (1) creating a strong team structure that will instinctively "close ranks" in the face of sudden adversity, and (2) preparing a composed response to any catastrophic situation. *Scholastic Coach* magazine published an interesting and informative article on this subject in its January, 1985 issue. Written by Joseph M. Puggelli of the McBurney School in New York City, it is one of the more pertinent writings on this subject relating to a football program that I have read. It contains valuable recommendations which can be of great use to you in structuring your own plan for preparing for catastrophe.

Meeting #2, the meeting with your support staff, should include the following items on its agenda:

1. Assign summer and preseason duties (i.e. taking inventory, organizing, restocking, repairing and/or replacing all

required equipment and supplies) to all staff members based on their positions.

2. Arrange for the team doctor(s) and all trainers to set up a proper training/therapy room and to conduct team physical examinations before practice.
3. Outline field care procedures for all practice and playing fields with the student field manager and school grounds-keeper.
4. Set up computerized scouting program procedures with the teacher, student, or parent who will supervise this program. This may require a separate short meeting to decide on additional hardware and/or software that may be required.

More and more high schools throughout the country are adding computer courses to their curricula. Many schools possess several table-top computer units and teach a sophisticated range of study. If your school has this capacity, make arrangements with the teacher of these courses to set up a computerized scouting program. In most instances a quality desk-top computer can handle basic computer scouting requirements, and programs can easily be set up to receive information in the coach's own terminology. Enter into the computer these ten pieces of scouting information for each offensive play: play number, yardline, down, yards to go, run or pass, formation, play, ball carrier, hole number, and yards gained. Within minutes a plethora of valuable specific information will be available. Formation recurrence, play recurrence, ball carrier recurrence, formation-play recurrence, play/ball carrier recurrence, down and distance-formation recurrence, down and distance-formation play recurrence and yardline-play recurrence can all be programmed from those simple ten pieces of information. The more games that are available for computer analysis, the more accurate the tendency predictions will be. Have your computer expert work out the details based on the type of computer he or she will be using and the amount of information you require.

Your third meeting, the meeting with school officials, should include the following agenda items:

1. Present and discuss your priorities and practice plans.
2. Present the schedule for the summer conditioning program, and for the summer and preseason practice sched-

ules, and obtain all legal and technical clearances for the use of school facilities.

3. Schedule physical examination dates for players as previously discussed with team doctor(s) and trainers. The school nurse should also be included as part of the medical team in attendance at the physical examinations.

4. Request that arrangements be made with local hospitals, emergency clinics, paramedics, and ambulance facilities for prompt response and accurate care in any medical emergency situation throughout the summer and regular season.

5. Clarify all conditions and situations relating to medical and liability insurance. Request that information be sent to all players, coaches, and staff regarding the extent and limitations of insurance maintained by the school and/or district.

6. Request that arrangements be made with the school photographer for team and individual photos, and that the date for these photo sessions be scheduled during preseason practice and announced prior to the start of summer vacation.

7. Request that arrangements be made for proper transportation as required during the summer recess and/or regular season.

Making proper arrangements for transportation may appear routine; however, it can have a significant effect on your program. The key word is *proper*. I have found, for instance, that bus rides over 40 minutes in length on a school bus can have an adverse effect, mentally and physically, on players and coaches. The seats are uncomfortable and the ride is rough and tiresome. It becomes difficult to regain one's concentration and physical dexterity after a long, uncomfortable bus ride. Although it may seem to be a minor factor, I have witnessed the negative impact of such a ride on the outcome of a game: It can significantly impair the first-half performances of both players and coaches, and may also afford a tangible edge to your opponents. I suggest that, before making arrangements for transportation, you thoroughly analyze the summer, preseason, and regular season schedules. Consider the distance to be traveled for each away game, the game time, the dressing and training facilities available. Request that arrangements be made for special coach buses with individual, comfortable seats, to be used on all trips longer than 40 minutes. Also arrange for a separate van or minibus to transport ahead of the team the head trainer, equipment manager, field manager, and a custodian to regular season games (see chapter 10 for details).

Summer Development and Practice

Before your players leave for their summer vacations, make sure they have specific information and dates for summer and preseason activities. Try to allow at least three weeks after the last day of school before beginning any summer activities. This will afford you, your players, and your staff an opportunity to revitalize your energies and clear your minds for the challenge of pursuing an excellent season.

Because summer is generally thought of as a time of leisure and relaxation, many highly successful high school coaches have discovered that their summer programs become more attractive, and hence more successful, when they approach them in a relaxed and recreational manner. There are many summer activities that are quite compatible with this approach. The summer conditioning maintenance program, as described in chapter 8, can be conducted as a competition in much the same manner as the off-season weight lifting program. Passing leagues and tournaments have obvious potential for fun-oriented approaches. Holding a few casual team get-togethers during the summer (barbecues, pizza parties, etc.) can have a unifying effect on your team's summer efforts, and summertime fund-raising events such as golf tournaments, tennis tournaments, distance runs, and cook-outs also set a pleasant tone for summer activities. You will need to spend time with the parent and booster groups arranging these fund-raising activities, as well as planning fall fund-raising events, so you might as well enjoy it!

There are also many informal, football-related activities that a coach can become involved in during the summer months. Some things I have always enjoyed doing for myself during the summer are attending summer coaching clinics, visiting local major colleges and professional preseason training camps, and attending sports medicine symposiums conducted by major local hospitals. Each of these activities, though informal in nature, generally yields a few gems of information that can be useful during the season ahead.

Camp Week and Preseason Practice

As the summer vacation nears its end and the beginning of preseason practice approaches, you should plan to schedule staff meetings with the purpose of reaffirming each staff member's understanding of his or her responsibilities during the preseason practice. On the evening preceding the first day of preseason practice, a meeting of all staff and players should be held and conducted solely by you, as varsity head coach. This general meeting should briefly cover a broad range of subjects: coaching and support staff introductions; rules for discipline; your position on smoking, alcohol, and drugs; your expectations and goals for the team; and the distribution of playbooks to all varsity players for study. Finally, you might take this opportunity to explain the foundation on which your program is based. If you agree with the precepts detailed in this book, that foundation will be the "pursuit of excellence"—the idea that everyone, working within a team structure, maintains a constant personal desire to improve. At the end of the general meeting, the players should be divided into groups according to division—varsity, junior varsity, freshman and so on. Each group meeting will be conducted by its own division head coach and staff, with each division leader discussing the conditions and circumstances unique to the division's team, and allowing a brief period for questions from the players.

The first week of preseason practice, in most parts of the country, is a combination of the teaching of basic fundamentals and conditioning. This physically demanding period is often referred to as "Hell Week" or "Crunch Week." But there is another approach to this conditioning/teaching period that is just now beginning to gain popularity among high school coaches, although it has been used in several different forms for some time. Often called "Camp Week," it is for all intents and purposes an amateur version of professional football's preseason camp. As the name implies, Camp Week is a residence activity for varsity players. This approach is designed to achieve all the positive goals of any "Hell Week," but at the same time reap a multitude of benefits not possible in a nonresidence situation. And it does all this in a pleasant, exciting, recreational atmosphere highly conducive to concentration and motivation.

The details of Camp Week vary from place to place, to a large degree dependent upon school, district, or conference restrictions. High school football federations in most areas of the country require that Camp Week not be funded by school or booster groups. Most programs establish a minimum daily charge for each player to cover the cost of food and beverage. To keep the program manageable, it is usually reserved for the varsity team only. The football players, as well as the coaches, trainers, manager, and equipment manager, establish residency on the high school campus for the entire conditioning/teaching week. The players move their bedding and some personal belongings into the gymnasium or a group of small classrooms or a general assembly room—whatever area is close to showers and toilet facilities. The coaches and staff move into adjacent rooms, close enough to monitor the players without being ever-present. Quite often, the players' fathers and brothers help them move in and set up in dormitory fashion. Some fathers volunteer to be dorm monitors—if a man's personality and relationship with his son are positive and pleasant enough to fill this role, take advantage of the offer to free yourself and your staff for evening meetings. Mothers and sisters readily volunteer to help prepare and serve meals. This special week has an unusually unifying effect on the entire school community. Everyone—parents, players, coaches, and staff—works together to get to know one another on a different, more personal level.

The more obvious benefits of the program are the elimination of several problems, including transportation problems, missed practices, and tardiness, and the control of several important factors such as proper diet and sufficient time for rest and relaxation. Also, Camp Week requires a commitment of time that results in a unique bond between players and staff that only living together can create.

Table 9.1 depicts a typical day's schedules of activities during Camp Week.

The daily routine varies only during the last 1 1/4 hours of the afternoon practice (3:45 to 5:00), and in the "special emphasis" practice during the midday session. These changes are based solely on what you determine requires work on any given day. The week culminates on Saturday morning with an offense-defense scrimmage after an extended stretching, flexibility, warm-

Table 9.1 Camp Week Daily Schedule

Day _____ Monday _____ Date _____ 17 August 1987 _____

TIME	ACTIVITY	SPECIFICS
6:45 A.M.	Wake-up call	Personal hygiene
7:15 A.M.	Breakfast	Nutritionally balanced as recommended by team doctor
8:00 A.M.	Injury and health check	Head trainer to evaluate and treat complaints
8:30 A.M.	Group meetings (offense)	Head coach and assistants to discuss day's practice goals
9:00 A.M.	Practice (shorts, shirts, shoes)	Stretching, aerobics, flexibility
10:00 A.M.	''	Agility drills, footwork, jumping rope
11:00 A.M.	Shower	Personal hygiene and dress for lunch
11:30 A.M.	Lunch	Nutritionally balanced as recommended by team doctor
12:15 P.M.	Rest period	
1:00 P.M.	Injury and health check	Head trainer to evaluate and treat complaints
1:30 P.M.	Special emphasis practice	Technique practice for individual position(s) as required
2:00 P.M.	Group meetings (defense)	Head coach and assistants to discuss day's practice goals
3:00 P.M.	Practice (full equipment)	Stretching and flexibility
3:30 P.M.	''	Form running, agility drills
3:45 P.M.	''	Contact drills by position
4:15 P.M.	''	Group/team techniques and mechanics
4:45 P.M.	''	Light scrimmage
5:00 P.M.	Shower	Personal hygiene and dress for dinner
5:45 P.M.	Injury and health check	Head trainer to evaluate and treat complaints

Table 9.1 Cont.

TIME	ACTIVITY	SPECIFICS
6:00 P.M. Dinner		Nutritionally balanced as recommended by team doctor
7:30 P.M. Personal and social activities		General relaxation activities (T.V., special movie, ping pong, etc.)
9:00 P.M. Evening snack		Fresh fruit, popcorn, granola bars, etc.—no candy
10:30 P.M. Lights out		

up period. Parents and friends are invited to attend the scrimmage and a cookout lunch that follows. After lunch everyone packs up bedding and belongings and returns home.

It is a week of healthy conditioning, and because of the positive learning atmosphere, the players will absorb more of the football fundamentals than they otherwise might. During this week, the players are also encouraged to see each other as individuals. They are taught responsibility, discipline, and hard work; they learn that other people depend upon them, and they learn whom they can depend upon. Camp Week is a technique that is highly recommended by some of the best and most successful high school coaches in the country, and is worthy of your serious investigation. It can be developed into a strong positive tradition, helpful to any coach in building a strong program.

After a sound start to your preseason with the proper conditioning period, the remaining weeks of the preseason will progress rapidly. At first, two-a-day practice sessions will allow you to place concentrated emphasis on offense and the offensive kicking game in one session, and on defense and the defensive kicking game in the other session. If these double session practices are carefully organized, they can yield spectacular results. Other than the specific teaching of your Xs and Os, the following exercises will produce valuable information for player and team evaluations.

Offensive Practice—

- Stretching, flexibility and agility drills.
- Form running and timing. Distances should be 10 yds., 20 yds., and 40 yds. For meaningful evaluation, use times in 10 yds. and 20 yds. for linemen; times in 20 yds. and 40 yds. for linebackers and tight ends; times in 40 yds. and over for running backs, receivers, and defensive backs. Do not use the same running distance as a criterion for everyone.
- Concentration drill. Set up as many complete offensive units as your personnel permits. One unit at a time will line up at the 20-yd. line going toward the near goal. Send a play into the huddle of each unit in turn, using a different "snap" count. Position all your assistant coaches so that they can observe and grade each of their players on ability to concentrate on their primary assignment, technique, "snap" count release, and secondary assignment. Every play should be run from the 20-yd. line (against air) into the end zone; then the unit should run back to an assembly area behind the next huddle. This drill should be run near the beginning and at the end of each offensive practice for approximately 12 minutes. During the concentration drill at the end of practice you can add some defensive distractions, such as audibles, line movement, and so on.
- Automatic substitution. At the beginning of each offensive practice, read the personnel depth chart for each position. When you come together for "team" offense, keep the substitutes on one sideline. Regularly send a player out of the working unit to allow his immediate replacement to substitute without being called.

Defensive Practice—

- Stretching, flexibility, and agility drills.
- Pursuit drills. There are many different types of these drills outlined in the books and periodicals. Their aim is the same: Get as many men to the ball as quickly as possible. Research and find a drill that suits your team's personality best.
- Tackling drills. Make a point of including sideline, head-on, and open field tackling drills in every defensive practice. Research the proper mechanics and coaching techniques. Be

sure to teach both "hat across the ball" and "second man to the ball" techniques in your daily routine.

- Automatic substitution. Using the same procedure as on offense, make this a regular feature of your team defense practice.

Hold a regular brief coaches'meeting at the close of each practice, particularly during the double session period. Discuss all position development and daily individual and team progress, and address all problem areas with an eye toward solutions. At the end of each week, hold a precisely scripted scrimmage where each offensive play you run is numbered in sequence and run against a specific defensive scheme that you request. Conversely, the same procedure should be used for defense. At a weekly coaches' meeting after each scrimmage, discuss each player's performance, progress, attitude, and demeanor. Analyze team performance by reviewing the scripts and results of each play. Take notes on the adjustments recommended by your assistant coaches. The day after the scrimmage, you should evaluate all the notes taken at your weekly coaches' meeting. Realign personnel if needed, make adjustments, and reappraise your situation.

By the end of the double session period you should have the answers to two key questions: (1) What can we expect to execute well, immediately? and (2) How much more can we expect to execute properly by midseason? At that point, you can concentrate on those things you do well and work on the things you expect to accomplish eventually. It will be possible to outline in minute detail a progressive practice schedule for the single practice sessions through the remainder of the preseason.

Meet regularly with your staff throughout the balance of the preseason. Continue the individual and team evaluations and outline regular season practice and game day duties. You and your staff should select special assignment leaders for such things as drills and exercises. Select your leaders carefully; using the guidelines for leadership outlined in chapter 1, select young men who have a predisposition for these qualities. Work with these young men to develop their leadership qualities and encourage them to seek out and help other players to develop who may be future leaders.

Hold a special end-of-preseason award meeting to present special awards and citations to those players who showed outstanding courage, discipline, desire, hard work, determination, spirit, and dedication during the demanding preseason. This is a positive note and an incentive to help your program lead into the regular season and prepare for your first conference game.

Some conferences hold early-season games that are considered practice games and do not count toward the overall record in the league standings. Some conferences allow preseason scrimmages, and still others consider every game as a factor in the league standings. You will have to determine when your preseason ends and regular season practice begins. As a rule of thumb, I recommend that this transition be made 10 to 14 days prior to the first game that "counts."

Chapter 10

Preparing for the Game

Collect Scouting Data for Computer Analysis

The transition between the preseason and the regular season should be accented by a distinct change of routine and emphasis. In order to pursue excellence on the football field, it is important that the mental part of the game be dealt with completely and efficiently. Organize your week to include development of the players' proper mental approach to (a) the game, (b) their positions, and (c) the next opponent they will face. Before anyone can begin mental preparation for a new assignment (and each game is a new assignment), the mind must first be cleared of all other matters and totally focused on the task ahead. To accomplish this, you must forget the successes or failures of previous weeks and games, and you must do so as quickly as possible.

Scouting your opponents' games is another important part of being well-prepared. Future opponents may play some of their games on Saturday afternoon or Saturday evening. Some assistant coaches should be assigned to scout Saturday afternoon games, and you should scout Saturday evening games or any opponent's games that do not conflict with your regular preparation schedule. Lower division coaches should be used to scout games that you or your varsity staff cannot attend. All scouting personnel should use the same format in collecting scouting data. I have found that using a small tape recorder is the most efficient way to gather the most complete scouting information, particularly that which is required by a computerized scouting program (see chapter 9).

On Thursday of each week, eight days prior to every game, submit all scouting data to the head of your computerized scouting program. Request that he present the computer printout to you with a brief typewritten summary of information on extraordinary tendencies and outstanding individual performances of your next opponent. This report and printout should be in your hands by noon on Friday.

Review and Evaluate
Last Game Performance

In chapter 4 I recommended that you make every effort to schedule as many of your games as possible on Friday evenings instead of Saturday afternoons or evenings. The practice schedules in this chapter are based on a schedule of Friday evening games so that you may take full advantage of your extra day (Saturday) to begin your mental preparations for the week ahead. On Saturday morning following each game, hold a staff meeting to review the game films of the night before, grade each players' performance, and fill out individual evaluation sheets noting strong and weak points of performance for each player's benefit and future improvement. Over lunch with your coaching staff, quickly review the scouting report on your next opponent. Let everyone think about setting priorities and making adjustments until you meet as a staff again later in the day.

All players should report to campus each Saturday at 1:00 p.m. Have your team doctor and trainer check all injuries at this time, however minor they may seem, and arrange for proper treatment and/or therapy. After the physical check-ups, meet with the players to briefly review the films of last night's game. Hand out the graded performance sheets that you and your staff have prepared for each player, present awards to outstanding players, and discuss ways to improve overall performance in the future.

Develop Your Game Plan

Now that you have put past events behind, you are ready for the task ahead. Conclude your players' meeting with a synopsis of information about next week's opponent and briefly break into groups, headed by assistant coaches, to discuss general priorities for the next week of practice. The players' meetings should conclude by 3:00 p.m., with a solid transition from emphasis on past performance to emphasis on present challenge.

Saturday afternoon between 3:00 p.m. and 6:00 p.m. will allow you and your staff time to formulate a fundamental game plan, offensively and defensively. If possible, request that your league film be broken down into one roll of offense and one roll of defense. If this is not possible, the next most efficient approach is to swap halves of the game between your offensive staff and your defensive staff. After a short meeting with the entire staff outlining a basic approach for this game, separate your staff into two groups: offense headed by the offensive coordinator, and defense headed by the defensive coordinator. Give each coordinator the appropriate scouting report, computer printout, and game films to use in their meeting. Each group should then begin to formulate a game plan based on the answers to the following five questions:

1. What are the strengths and weaknesses of your opponent?
2. What do you already have in your offense/defense that can neutralize their strengths and exploit their weaknesses?
3. What must you add to your offense/defense/kicking game to beat this opponent?
4. Can you add these elements in a simple enough manner for everyone to learn and properly execute within the week?
5. To which "gimmick series" already in your playbook will this opponent be most vulnerable?

After the prospective coaching units arrive at solutions to these questions, you should meet with each, in turn, to solidify a basic game plan.

The next step is to have the offensive coaching unit and the defensive coaching unit view the opponents' game films separately. Each coach should make his own notes about the other team, paying specific attention to the opponents' mechanics and techniques and to individual outstanding athletes. Beyond understanding the general game plan, each position coach must prepare his players for the one-on-one challenge of the game. He must get each of his athletes ready to be successful against whatever type of player he will meet. Once the film session has ended, each coach should be expected to present his own views on the particular problems, if any, that the proposed game plan may cause for him. The coordinators should make note of these anticipated problem areas so that they may discuss them with you at a separate meeting on Monday morning. These meetings should conclude about 6:00 p.m. with a presentation by each unit coordinator of their tentative game plans for offense and defense.

If your games are played on Friday evenings, Sunday can be a day of rest for your entire staff. If your games are played on Saturday, the process described above must be accomplished on Sunday and there will be no day of rest. Regardless of the schedule, you must spend some time reviewing the game plans drawn up by your staff, with a mind to obviating any problems. You also must formulate a special team plan for the game.

Monday morning you should hold a short meeting with your coordinators to finalize the game plans and examine the problem areas anticipated by the position coaches. At the conclusion of this meeting a formal game plan should be drawn, typed, copied, and distributed to the entire coaching staff before practice. Use whatever format you wish, but be sure to include *all* information that you plan to cover in practices regarding plays, defenses, coaching points, personnel, formations, and so on.

If you are fortunate enough to have a last-period P.E. course available to you for your varsity football, use it for meetings, taping, and dressing. Many of the successful high school coaches that I have spoken with feel it is important to get to the players as soon as possible any material pertaining to the game. With this thought in mind, the first event of the new practice week might well be a team meeting briefly reviewing the scouting report and outlining the game plans for the week.

It is extremely important to assemble a scout team that consists of a blend of rookies and veterans that can most effectively simulate the upcoming opponents' offense and defense. This coalition should consist of tough, spirited athletes who are either specialists on one side of the line or inexperienced reserves with talent and enthusiasm. The depth of personnel and team size will have a profound effect on the makeup of this unit. However, try to assemble a group of 18 to 20 players who comprise a permanent scout unit, and who truly understand the value of their contribution to the team.

Plan and Execute Precise Practice Schedules

Each day before practice you must draw up and reproduce a practice schedule for that day. Most coaches prefer to use a schedule based on five-minute intervals, which divides a two-hour practice into 24 time segments. Each phase of practice will then be 5, 10, 15, 20, 25, or 30 minutes in length, based upon what you determine is required. Use the "practice outline chart" (see Table 10.1) as a guide to developing your own daily practice plan and reproduce a copy for each assistant coach, the head trainer, and the team manager.

Please note that this chart does not indicate a separate time for a "water break." In the past, I have found that it is more beneficial to the players that the team manager and his assistants make water and thirst quencher drinks available during the team periods in practice—on the sideline and in huddles. This also helps the pace of practice and does not interrupt concentration like a scheduled break always does.

Monday prepractice, a twenty-minute period before the start of formal practice, should consist of only a scout team practice conducted by one offensive assistant and one defensive assistant. These assistant coaches in charge of the scout team must prepare your opponent's offensive plays and defensive sets on large white cards (approximately 11" x 17") for easy viewing in a huddle. During this prepractice period, the coaches should familiarize the team with your opponent's most successful plays and formations, which is what your team must see during Monday practice. Assuming your school schedule allows for formal

Table 10.1 Practice Outline Chart

DAY: _____ Monday _____ DATE: _____ 7 Sept. 1987

PRACTICE TIME IN FIVE MINUTE SEGMENTS

PRACTICE ACTIVITY OR EMPHASIS	PRE	FIRST HOUR		SECOND HOUR		POST
WARM UP: Stretching and flexibility						
FORM RUNNING						
CONCENTRATION DRILL						
OFFENSIVE GROUP: Backs, Receivers, Line		D. Sets Off G/P				
OFFENSIVE TEAM		Dummy vs. Scout				
PURSUIT DRILL						

	O. Plays / Def. G/P	Dummy vs. Scout		K.O. / Saf. K.			Scout Team	Kickers / Punters
DEFENSIVE GROUP: Line, Linebackers, Backs								
DEFENSIVE TEAM								
SPECIAL TEAM: Offensive Kicking								
SPECIAL TEAM: Defensive Kicking								
TWO-MINUTE DRILL								
CATASTROPHE DRILL								
SPECIALIST								

practice to start at 3:00 p.m. during the regular season, a week's practice schedule might look something like this:

MONDAY (Sweats, helmets, shoes)

3:00—   Stretching and flexibility exercises

3:20—   Form running

3:25—   Concentration drill

3:30—   Offensive group

3:45—   Offensive team against scout defense

4:00—   Pursuit drill

4:05—   Defensive group

4:20—   Defensive team against scout offense

4:35—   Catastrophe drills/two-minute drills

4:45—   Kick-off/safety kick

5:00—   Kickers and punters—special instruction after practice

TUESDAY (Full equipment)

3:00—   Stretching and flexibility exercises

3:20—   Form running

3:25—   Concentration drill

3:30—   Offensive group (including form blocking)

3:45—   Offensive team—full contact against scout defense

4:00—   Pursuit drill

4:05—   Team form tackling

4:15—   Defensive group

4:30—   Defensive team—full contact against scout offense

4:45—   Catastrophe drills/two-minute drills

4:55—   Punt/P.A.T.

5:10—   Kickers, punters, long-snap centers and holders special instruction after practice

WEDNESDAY (Full equipment)

3:00—   Stretching and flexibility exercises

3:20—   Form running

3:25—   Concentration drill

3:30—   Offensive group (including form blocking)

3:45—   Offensive team—full contact against scout defense

4:00—   Pursuit drill

4:05—   Team form tackling

4:15—   Defensive group

4:30—   Defensive team—full contact against scout offense

4:45—   Catastrophe drills/two-minute drills

4:55—   Kick-off return/punt return

5:10—   Kickers, punters, long-snap centers and holders
         special instruction after practice

THURSDAY (Sweats, helmets, shoes, and game jerseys)

3:00—   Pregame ritual and stretching

3:20—   Concentration drill

3:30—   Two-minute offense against scout defense

3:45—   Two-minute defense against scout offense

4:00—   Review special teams

4:30—   "Game" with automatic sideline substitutions

4:50—   Catastrophe drills

Using this practice schedule as a guide, the following daily meeting and prepractice schedule will complement it properly:

MONDAY
(Previously outlined)

TUESDAY
Meetings: by position with film as required.
Prepractice: scout team, quarterbacks, receivers, defensive backs,
         linebackers (7 on 7 drills).

WEDNESDAY
Meetings: by position with film as required.
Prepractice: quarterbacks, receivers, centers, defensive backs,
         linebackers (7 on 7 drills).

THURSDAY
Meetings: team-review of objectives.
Prepractice: Pregame specialist warm-up.

Some general suggestions that might help to keep your practices efficient and productive:

- Be prepared. You and your assistants must know what you will be working on every minute of practice.
- Keep it simple. Make sure your instructions are direct and easy to understand by the players.
- Work on execution. Concentrate daily on precise technique and mechanics to continually reduce the margin for error.
- Communicate. Constantly check your communication skills by asking your players to confirm your instructions.
- Motivate. Convey your own enthusiasm and confidence to your players throughout every practice.
- Keep things moving. Run from one phase of practice to another and use constant running during daily team drill periods for conditioning.

Develop Pregame Ritual

In addition to your normal warm-up procedures, you should develop a special, inspirational pregame warm-up ritual. Every year I see several unique concepts for pregame rituals that help inspire teams to open their game with a positive thrust. Some use drill team precision exercises, others a "silent" drill, and one even had their school band play "Conquest" to the team in a closed locker room. Find some distinctive approach to your pregame ritual that reflects your team's personality. Practice this ritual on Thursday and as often as your schedule permits before the game.

Meet briefly before practice each day with your assistant coaches to hand out and explain the daily practice schedule. Schedule a regular post-practice coaches' meeting on Monday to discuss adjustments in the game plan, and on Thursday to discuss game-day procedures and responsibilities.

To be absolutely certain that your support staff understand and are prepared for their game-day responsibilities, schedule a regular Friday morning meeting with the head trainer, the team manager, the equipment manager, and the field manager.

Review their general responsibilities and note any special conditions or circumstances unique to this particular game. All support staff personnel indicated in the following paragraphs must understand and execute their game-day duties to prevent pregame panic and sideline confusion.

The head trainer must organize his or her assistants for pregame therapy, pregame taping, sideline procedures, and responsibilities. For all away games, the trainer must pack and transport all supplies and arrive ahead of the team. He or she is also responsible for preparing a proper taping area in the locker room, and setting up an examination area and emergency procedures for the sideline.

The team manager must prepare "the box" (a trunk mounted on wheels that contains basic supplies and equipment). He or she is responsible for the availability and proper condition of all required playing and support gear (balls, kicking tees, towels, water bottles, cleat scrapers, etc.). For away games, the team manager is responsible for seeing that all players' personal gear is packed and transported to and from the game on the team bus.

The equipment manager must organize his or her assistants to check all playing equipment (pads, helmets, shoes, socks, uniforms, etc.). For all away games, the equipment manager must pack and transport all repair tools and supplies and arrive ahead of the team. He or she is required to set up an equipment repair area on the sideline and isolate an area in the locker room for collecting soiled game uniforms, towels, and so forth.

The field manager must prepare the sidelines at both home and away games. Coaches' field and booth headphones, benches, tables, chains and down markers, operators, and the time clock are all his or her responsibility. For away games, the field manager must pack and transport communication gear, tables, and examining bench and arrive ahead of the team. He must prepare the team's sideline and examine the field and facilities for flaws, reporting these conditions to you upon your arrival with the team.

All other personnel should have been apprised of their duties during the preseason, with the possible exception of a regular school custodian. The administration should assign a regular custodian to be responsible for maintaining clean locker rooms for visiting teams at home games. Also, the custodian must pack and transport cleaning equipment and supplies to away game sites. He must arrive ahead of the team to be sure locker and dressing facilities are clean. After your away games, he will be responsible, together with the field manager and equipment manager, for cleaning your locker room—leaving it cleaner than it was when you arrived.

Pregame Activities

In most areas, varsity football games that are played on Friday evenings kick off at approximately 7:30 p.m. If you can make arrangements with your school, and if your conference has no restrictions against it, schedule a team meal in the school cafeteria for approximately 3:30 p.m. (four hours before game time) on Friday. Many nutrition experts recommend a pregame meal high in complex carbohydrates—check with your own nutrition expert for specific menu ideas.

The team meal should be followed by a rest/relaxation period. An excellent form of relaxation prior to home games is the showing of a rented film in the school auditorium. Assembling the team in the auditorium for a film also allows you to conduct a brief team meeting immediately afterward, before dressing and preparing for the game. Prior to away games, a short football film (such as a half-hour NFL highlight film) allows for a brief period of relaxation before packing gear and traveling.

Whether at home or away, the team must start taping and dressing at least 1 1/2 hours before kickoff. Anyone requiring pregame therapy should get into the locker room a bit earlier. Assistant and student trainers, under the supervision of the head trainer, should do all the normal preventative taping. The head trainer must personally handle the taping of all injuries. The taping/dressing period is an excellent opportunity for the players to begin a concentration and visualization process that many coaches feel is imperative to a good performance.

If a player—or if anyone for that matter—creates a regular ritual for entering into a state of concentration, it is a subtle form of self-hypnosis. The simple act of sitting on a taping bench, or putting on a girdle pad, or tying a shoe, can become a trigger mechanism for concentration. Work with your players to find that trigger during this preparation period. Teach them how to concentrate on their assignments. Emphasize the use of visualization, having each player visualize all of the moves that he has already seen his opponent make on game films. If your player concentrates on facing his opponent, one-on-one, he will be able to visualize continued successes. Hypnotists believe that the mind cannot distinguish between an imagined and an actual experience. If this is so, then every imagined success a player has helps to build confidence so that real success can be achieved.

Send your "early outs"—passers, receivers, kickers, punters, and long-snappers—onto the field (usually behind one end zone) with approximately five minutes left in the preliminary game. Have them throw, catch, and run easily to get their shoulders, elbows, hips, knees, and ankles loose and supple. As soon as the field is clear after the lower division game, bring the rest of the team onto the field and begin your pregame ritual. This ritual should be carefully timed to end seven minutes before the scheduled kickoff.

Take your team into the locker room for a few minutes to relax and receive any last minute instructions or adjustments you feel are necessary. Send your captains out to the field for the coin toss when the referee calls for them, and *you* lead the team onto the field just one minute before kickoff.

Chapter 11

Coaching the Game

Develop a Visceral Feel for the Game

In the nearly 40 years that I have been involved with football as a player, coach, and observer, one aspect of the game has genuinely puzzled me. What is there about coaching the game that can change a man's personality, particularly that of the head coach? Over the years I have seen a great number of mild-mannered Coach Jekylls turn into maniacal Coach Hydes in the time it takes to walk from the locker room to the field. I'm not talking about the coach who is always a maniac, or the coach who becomes incensed by poor officiating. I am talking about a coach who, during the week, is a compassionate man with a friendly manner and a good sense of humor, and who makes a sudden metamorphosis into a raging, unfeeling, insensitive crazy-man on the sidelines during a game.

My curiosity about this phenomenon has led to considerable research on my part, with many hours of reading, studying, and discussing the subject with doctors, psychologists, and other coaches. Although there does not seem to be a clear consensus on the precise cause, there is strong evidence leading to the theory that such behavior stems from panic, probably due to a hidden insecurity about one's basic ability. This evidence is supported by the frequent observation that this particular phenomenon is not something that happens to coaches who have developed a visceral feel for the game. Therefore, a rather simplistic way to obviate this syndrome would be to become a student of the game.

Learn as much as you can about what you are doing; experiment with your own theories and those of others in the field whom you respect. Develop a total understanding of the causes and effects and motivations of the game of football. In short, work to develop a visceral feel for the game. If you understand football this well, you will naturally bring the following elements to the sidelines with you:

Vision—to see and foresee action
Intrepidity—to boldly use your imagination
Self-confidence and poise—to maintain emotional stability
Communication—to effectively exchange information
Execution—to effectively pursue predetermined goals
Respect—to sustain the feeling of team togetherness
Analysis—to maintain flexibility and a readiness to adjust
Love of the game—to stimulate motivation in others

This dedication and leadership on your part will instill within your players and staff a positive, confident, winning attitude—a solid foundation for success.

Organize Your Sideline

With your demeanor on the sideline under control, your next job is to organize your sideline. First, you need to evaluate the members of your coaching staff in terms of their best abilities for contributing to the overall success of the team. Second, position your sideline staff and assign each of them specific game responsibilities that take maximum advantage of their abilities. For instance, assistant coaches who possess strong visualizing and analytical skills might be of great benefit to the effective execution of any game plan if they were located in the booth during the game. The booth would afford them the opportunity for an optimum view of the action, and thus information relayed to the head coach over the field phones would have a much greater impact on his ability to make valid coaching decisions. On the other hand, if there are some assistant coaches who possess exceptional communication skills, these men should be on the sidelines with the team; they will be most effective in relaying accurate and complete information from head coach to players.

Depending, of course, upon the size and makeup of your staff, the following game responsibilities should be assigned to specific individuals:

1. *Offensive Signal Caller.* Sends plays in to quarterback by means of shuttling players or hand signals. Call the plays from some sort of script (a list of plays from your playbook selected especially for each game and practiced intensely all week). Communicate with booth coaches constantly for vital data to aid in play selection and in-game adjustments.

2. *Defensive Signal Caller.* Send plays into defensive captain by hand signals or substitution of special situation players. Call the defenses from a situation chart prepared from computer-scouting data and play recurrence information. Communicate with booth coaches constantly for updates on game data to aid in defensive adjustments.

3. *Booth Coaches.* Keep in constant touch by field phone with head coach and signal callers. The first information to communicate to the sidelines during each play, and as soon as possible is: (a) down, (b) distance, (c) location on field, and (d) yardline. Quickly forward any additional information requested, plus any observations which may be pertinent to the execution of the game plan. Chart each offensive play and defense with particular attention to the degree of success. At halftime the staff will analyze this chart and make adjustments accordingly.

4. *Special Teams Coordinator.* Coordinate and call the kicking game, based on preplanned guidelines specifically designed with each opponent's strengths and weaknesses in mind. Keep the kicking units "at the ready," with proper instructions, prepared to execute as soon as they

take the field. (This allows the head coach time to decide his strategy without causing confusion and delays in the special team.)

5. *Sideline Adjustment Coaches (Offense and Defense).* Use chalkboard to relay and discuss adjustments in assignments or techniques to players on sidelines. Clarify ambiguities and correct mistakes when individual players or team units are off the field. Relay information from the head coach, coordinators, and booth coaches to players, which will eliminate shouting and confusion on the sidelines. (This assignment is usually given to a position coach who is familiar with all phases of the offense and/or defense.)

6. *Alerts Coach.* Working with the student stat keeper assigned to maintain "key factors" (see chapter 6), this coach will keep track of all vital general information. Time-outs remaining for each team, quarter, time left in quarter, injuries and availability of injured players, substitutions for injured players, and catastrophe procedures all fall under his area of responsibility. He should be near the head coach at all times to be ready with this information upon request or when apropos.

7. *Medical Team.* The head trainer should position himself at the 30-yard line closest to the placement of the ball (changing ends as the ball crosses the 50-yard line). The team doctor should stay in the general area of the examining table with an assistant trainer also in that vicinity. When an injury occurs, the head trainer must reach the player as soon as time has been called. As he starts onto the field, the alerts coach must call out "man down." This is the signal for the team doctor to come to the sidelines and watch the head trainer for a predetermined signal. The signal will indicate whether or not the doctor is required on the field. Once the injured player is on the sideline he should be taken directly to the examining table for a complete check by the doctor (no matter how minor the injury may seem). From this point, it is the team doctor's responsibility to evaluate the extent of the injury and determine if the player can return to the game. *The doctor's decision must be final* and should not be overruled, pressured, or influenced by any coach or parent. The team doctor should notify the alerts coach regarding the status of any injured player.

8. *Team Manager*. Responsible for organizing student staff on sideline. Water and "Gatorade" people must have constant supply—in cups on sideline, and in bottles to bring on field during time-outs. Towels should be kept available on sideline and on field during time-outs. An assistant manager should have cleat-cleaning pads strategically located for players' use, particularly in bad weather. Student staff must be assigned to attend kicking tees, footballs, oxygen, ice, and "the box." All of these assignments must be planned in advance with appropriate territories and stations prescribed by the manager.

9. *Equipment Manager*. Responsible for setting up a work area on the sidelines for emergency equipment repair. There also should be a limited supply of replacement jerseys, hard pads, helmets, face masks, soft pads, "flack jackets," cleats, and so forth on hand in the work area. Any player who has equipment problems will know exactly where to go for repairs or replacement.

10. *Stats Keepers*. Must keep an exact record of each offensive, defensive, or special teams play. Stats keepers should stay at the side of the play callers or coordinators at all times so that they can hear the play or defense being called and record the results quickly. Their notes should be clear so that coaches may use them for halftime analysis. After the game, the notes should be transcribed and typed in time for the Saturday morning coach's viewing of the game film.

As you may have guessed by now, my belief is that this type of sideline organization is designed to eliminate confusion, delay, and errors. To increase your sideline efficiency, consider having your support staff wear distinctly different outfits (i.e., trainers in white, managers in stripes, equipment manager in dark school color, etc.). The signal callers and head coach should also wear colors contrasting to the team jerseys—if the team wears white, the coaches should wear a dark color and vice versa.

Plan Game Procedures

Other elements of game procedures that require advanced thought and precise planning are: (1) two-minute offense and defense, (2) substitution patterns, (3) halftime routine, and (4) pre-second half on-field ritual. These procedures must be precisely defined and timed to be effective and to contribute to the team's success. They must be practiced regularly during the week, every week.

The two-minute offense and defense that you practice during the week must be based on your regular offense and defense as well as on the scouting data that you have compiled on your opponent. There are a few important suggestions that I would like to make with regard to your two-minute package. Be sure that you practice your offense by moving the ball from your 10-yard line to the opponent's 15-yard line and also into the end zone with 3 time outs, 2 time outs, and 1 time out. Set the clock at 2 minutes, 1 minute, and 45 seconds. Practice your defense in much the same manner, trying to keep the opponent's ball carrier inbounds to force time-outs and run out the clock. Also, practice "quick" set-ups on field goals and "quick" line-ups for a field goal block. I have seen high school, college, and professional teams lose games in the last few seconds because their "quick" kicking teams were not ready or failed to perform properly.

Put into action, for each game, a regular substitution pattern using as many players as possible. This will result in player enthusiasm, lift team morale, and, in the long run, help your overall program. I truly believe that a high school football coach must make every effort to encourage his players to be well-rounded football players, able to play several positions. This fosters a better understanding of the game, stimulates the learning process, and helps to create intelligent field leaders. Specialization is for insects, not young men!

Unfortunately, though, this is not always possible. There will be some players who, due to inexperience, immaturity, or lack of coordination, are very limited in their athletic abilities. In most programs, however, there will come a time when you will be required to play these young men. Perhaps the outcome of a game may hinge on their performance. You must find a way to develop the confidence of these players in order to increase their ability to perform, and what better way to do that than through game experience? *Everyone* can do *something* reasonably well. You and your coaching staff must make an effort to find out just what that something is with each one of your marginal players.

Perhaps a long-snapper or a good blocker for the PAT team is hiding among your lesser talented players. There may even be a punter or a placekicker. Many will be able to execute one particular special situation assignment (short yardage, nickel or dime defenses, field goal block, etc.). Try to find everyone's forte and use these players as much as possible in every game.

Regular Halftime Routine

As I have mentioned previously, routines are very important to a football team. A halftime routine should be established, and the same routine should be followed at every halftime. Whatever routine you decide is best for you, your coaching staff, and your players is fine. However, I strongly recommend that you begin your halftime routine, while the players are taking a brief rest and refreshment, with a coaches' meeting to review the first-half game plan and discuss adjustments. Once that is accomplished, any format you choose for talks, meetings, instructions, or chalkboard discussions can be accomplished quickly and efficiently. The information imparted to the players at halftime should be confined to corrections and adjustments that will allow you to maintain or regain control of the game. If at all possible, try to avoid angry outbursts unless they are specifically calculated to motivate the team. Controlled anger is sometimes an extremely effective tool in helping to stimulate a team into regaining its concentration and focus.

Following the regular halftime procedure, before the captains leave to go out on the field for the second-half instructions, prepare your team for the challenge ahead. Whether you are winning by 40 points or losing by 40 points should have no effect on what you challenge them to do. I firmly believe that the only meaningful challenge anyone can present to another person is to give all that is possible to give. In football, that means always to make one's best effort. This challenge can be presented in many ways, depending on who is doing the presenting, but it is the only concept that is truly consistent with the "pursuit of excellence." A great admiral of the U.S. Navy once observed, "There are no great men; there are only great challenges that ordinary men are forced by circumstances to meet." Those words are from the late Admiral William F. "Bull" Halsey, a daring and brilliant naval strategist in World War II who, incidentally, was an outstanding football player while attending the Naval Academy at Annapolis.

One minute after the captains go onto the field, lead the team out for a pregame stretch (this time may vary according to league or conference time regulations). In some unique presentation, quickly stretch leg and back muscles. This will help prevent major muscle pulls in the first few minutes of the second half, particularly if you come from a warm locker room to a cold field. You should now be ready to win the second half!

Chapter 12

After the Game

Regular After-Game Routine

One of the more difficult things for a new head coach to deal with is the problem of what to do after the game. Most coaches, veterans and rookies alike, generally get deeply involved in the game. For that reason, their reaction to a win or a loss is often exaggerated and sometimes even counterproductive to any kind of coaching exercise. A highly successful method of controlling and channeling these reactions is, once again, to establish a regular after-game routine. Although your individual personality will dictate exactly what you say and how you say it, I think it might be helpful here to illustrate the type of routine that should be followed in order to continue ''coaching'' after the game. Once the teams have completed their exchange of cordialities on the field, your team should return to the bench area of your sideline for a few brief observations from you about the game. Try to confine your sideline remarks to the kind of effort and performance given by the *team*. Let them know if their effort was outstanding, mediocre, or terrible, regardless of the score. Impress upon them your feeling about their team performance (was it "crisp" or "sloppy"?).

When your sideline meeting is over, have the team shower, dress, and report to unit meetings which should be conducted by the offensive, defensive, and special teams coordinators. While the players are in the locker room, meet with your assistant coaches regarding specifics to be discussed during these unit meetings: particular plays, players, techniques, and execution that were extraordinary or that desperately need work. Also, determine who will receive the game balls.

The unit meetings should be only 10 to 15 minutes long and will be far more successful if they are conducted in a relatively low-key manner, rather than in a highly charged atmosphere. If you have just won the game, the players' moods will be exuberant and they will be enthusiastic in their reactions to both praise and constructive criticism. But after a loss, the players' moods will be quite dejected, and it may take a controlled leader with a good sense of humor to be effective in conveying either praise or criticism.

While your coaching staff is conducting the unit meetings, you can take the time to meet with your team doctor and head trainer, after they have examined and evaluated the injured players, to discuss each preliminary prognosis and/or required therapy. You should also meet with your game photographer to make arrangements for exchange of game film with your next opponent and to discuss any problems that might have occurred during the filming of the game. Part of the game photographer's responsibility should be to have game film delivered to the processor for immediate development and picked up first thing Saturday morning in time for your coaches' meeting.

Before returning to the team, meet with newspaper reporters who have covered the game. Praise the efforts of your staff and players as much as possible, regardless of the outcome of the game. Accept full responsibility for a poor performance. Then meet briefly with your entire team and staff once again to award the game balls and make some parting comments.

Informal Get-Together With Coaches

Before leaving your office, look over the scouting report for your next opponent and take it home for further study before you go to bed. Make it a regular practice to conclude each game evening with an informal, short get-together with your coaches at your home or local restaurant. Although this may seem superficial and unnecessary, many coaches feel it has a solidifying effect on the staff and it affords anyone the opportunity to vent remaining frustrations in an atmosphere of good humor and fellowship. My own view is that, in addition to these benefits, it helps the coaching staff to "complete" their thinking about the game that was just played. As I have mentioned in chapter 11, before anyone can begin thinking about the challenge ahead, it is first necessary to stop dwelling on past efforts.

Proper coaching after the game can be a great help to your program. It fosters a feeling of togetherness among the coaching staff and players simply by continuing the coaching effort. This consistency in leadership binds the team together and reinforces the players' confidence in their coach as a man who truly cares about them.

Starting on Saturday morning (or the morning after your game day), begin preparing for your next game by repeating the procedures described in chapters 10 and 11.

Chapter 13

After the Season

The postseason for the head coach of any high school consists of five major activities:

- Player counseling, including meetings with seniors to discuss their continuing education and athletic scholarship possibilities
- Football Awards Banquet
- Meeting with coaching staff to discuss recommendations on adjustments in the program for next season
- Meeting with school administrators to request procedural improvements and establish the school budget for next year's program
- Meeting with booster groups to discuss next season's additional budget requirements and organize a schedule of off-season fund-raising events

Prepare for Player Counseling

If I had to select one of these as being the postseason activity that will have the most positive effect on a program in general, I would unhesitatingly choose player counseling. If this procedure is handled properly, it can dramatically underscore a head coach's sincerity as a leader who has true concern for the young men entrusted into his care.

Preparing for this counseling period requires some advanced research and investigation on your part. The first thing to do is set up a card file of as many colleges and universities as possible throughout the country that recruit high school football players. The name of each institution, kept in alphabetical order, should be typed on 5″ x 7″ cards. These cards can be color coded to instantly reflect the type of financial assistance the school is generally willing to give—full scholarship, tuition and books, tuition only, help in arranging for grants and aid, and so on. In addition to the proper name, address, and telephone number of the college or university, the file card should contain the following information:

- Name and contact information of local football recruiter
- Name and contact information of head coach
- Name and contact information of athletic counselor
- NCAA, CFA, NAIA (and so on) affiliation and division
- Academic rating, including the most highly rated major courses of study
- General information on quality of athletes enrolled (size, speed, strength, etc.)
- General information on the institution itself (size, location, type of campus, climatic conditions, etc.)

Since most high school coaches receive inquiry cards about their better players from major colleges at the beginning of each school year, it is relatively easy to keep records on these schools. Smaller colleges with smaller recruiting budgets require much more extensive inquiry to maintain accurate records. You can gather information on these smaller colleges, and on junior colleges, during coaching clinics and in various periodicals. These schools might be interested in your good football players who are not quite big enough or fast enough for the major colleges. There are literally hundreds of schools like this that can offer a quality education, and perhaps worthwhile financial aid packages, to some of your deserving and/or needy athletes.

During the season, contact some of these college recruiters directly, using your card file, to stimulate their curiosity about one player or another. Send them, on occasion, information, stats, newspaper clippings, and so forth, to keep them interested. Invite them to your home games when they are in the area. Try to get to know as many of them as possible. Work as hard at this as you would on any other part of your program preparation.

Now, after the season, you will be able to sit down with each one of your senior athletes and be prepared to help them with sound advice on where it might be possible to use their athletic skills to continue their education. If some of your senior players do not intend to play football beyond high school, you will still have valuable information for them, and, in concert with their high school academic counselor, can give them some of the help they need to choose a direction. After you have completed these senior counseling sessions, meet briefly with each of your underclass players to help them begin focusing on high school academic goals that will enhance their chances of attending a college of their choice. Assume that, with hard work and dedication, all of your athletes will be able to attend college. Help them to achieve this goal, whether or not they plan to continue playing football after high school.

Awards Banquet

The type, location, and scope of an awards banquet will vary depending upon the personality of each school, community, team, or head coach. There are, however, certain procedures that are necessary to run a successful awards banquet. The success of an awards activity can be measured only by the value it has vis-a-vis an overall football program, and it has value only if it is conducted in such a manner that it reinforces the *positive effort* of those who have given their best, those who have pursued excellence.

This recognition of positive effort should be as prominent in the awards ceremony as the recognition of outstanding athletic ability. It is particularly important that the graduating seniors be recognized for effort and ability in athletics, academics, and citizenship; I know from personal experience that if they are, the self-esteem that results will motivate them to future achievement. And successful alumni who are former football players are the best possible public relations advertisement any football program can have. Senior achievement awards, coupled with awards for outstanding underclassmen, all add up to an entertaining presentation that will spell success for your awards banquet.

Meet With Coaches and Administrators

After you have completed the player counseling and the awards banquet, you should schedule meetings with your coaching staff, the school administrators, and the school booster groups. The meeting with your coaching staff should concentrate on the major problems that the program encountered during the season, and should include frank discussion and evaluation of the causes of these problems, as well as recommendations for solutions. This meeting is intended to help you assess the season, and plan for changes and improvements in the immediate future. The information exchanged at this meeting is your way of insuring that the program continues to improve—use it positively in the off-season, while planning for the next season.

In meeting with the school administrators and athletic director, be prepared to discuss in convincing detail your budget requirements and any procedural improvements that you feel are necessary for the benefit of the program. Try to be as fiscally responsible and logical as possible, developing concepts that will save time, money, and aggravation rather than increase them. Try to evaluate problems as the administrators would, and present solutions that will help everyone. Do not be afraid to be progressive and innovative. However, don't just make suggestions for suggestion's sake—always keep in mind your ultimate goals for the program.

Meet With Parents and Booster Groups

Finally, arrange for a meeting, or a series of meetings, with parent and booster groups. Once again, in an organized, well-prepared presentation, discuss your plans, staff requirements, team goals, and any outside financial help that will be required for a successful season next year. Work with these groups planning off-season fund-raising events and promotions. Help them to help you! I am sure you will find these people to be fully supportive and anxious to help, if you cooperate with them.

Generally, the major portion of these postseason activities can be accomplished before the first of the year. This will allow you two to three months of relative relaxation in order to reenergize before your off-season activities begin (return to chapter 5 and start all over again).

Chapter 14

Points of Interest

There are very few occupations that still afford one the opportunity to teach positive, basic human values. Coaching amateur athletics in general, and coaching high school football in particular, still offer this challenge. As a head football coach in high school, you will have both the opportunity and the responsibility to meet this challenge. Most high school students are still somewhat insulated from such things as unethical legal and business practices, advocacy journalism, and self-serving political activism. You can make the difference between your athletes believing in themselves and their ability to control their own destinies, or not really believing in anything. As a coach you can teach, by example, that courage is not sickness, loyalty is not subservience, honesty is not callow, pride in achievement is not a sin, courtesy is not out of style, and imagination is not foolish fancy.

Above all else that comes to mind, the most important thing that coaches can teach their athletes is *maturity*. Maturity incorporates all of the leadership qualities and positive personal values described in the first two chapters of this book. Maturity is the major factor in success, in athletics as well as in "life its own-self" (to borrow a phrase from one of my favorite writers, Dan Jenkins). The development of maturity within an individual creates the two vital elements that are essential for true success. These elements are personal character and a sense of humor. The mature athlete is able to equate true success with effort, and can keep the successes he does achieve in proper perspective. The more mature your athletes, the more successful your program will be, and the more rewarding your own experience as a coach. But since this book is about the "pursuit of excellence" in building a high school football program, let us concentrate on the benefits to your program.

The reason that winning teams win and that successful high school football programs are consistently successful is quite simple—these programs develop maturity; they turn boys into young men. Whether by design or by instinct, the coaches who head these programs realize that maturity plays an important role in making a program successful. They have the ability to communicate the importance of this role to their players by their own example and by the example of their assistant coaches.

If you were to examine and analyze many of these successful programs as I have, I think you would clearly see the correlation between maturity and success. A successful high school football program will always include individuals with the following traits:

- *Head Coach*. He is the one person with enough knowledge and authority to set the pace for the rest of the people in his program. A successful coach is willing to "stick his neck out" and take calculated risks without fear and without shifting blame. He is willing to help motivate others.
- *Assistant Coaches*. The assistant coaches have confidence—without arrogance—in their own knowledge and ability. They possess the patience and determination that are necessary to teach precise technique and mechanics. They readily accept the challenges and responsibilities that the head coach requires of them.
- *Players*. Successful players work hard and pay close attention to their coaches. They are generally self-disciplined and self-motivated. They understand the importance of dedication and have developed a strong desire to be as good as they can be at what they do.

- *Support Staff.* Both the adult and student support staff are comprised of people who are proud of their assignments, no matter what they may be. They all know their jobs are an integral part of the team's success. A successful support staff member does more than what is required to get the job done.

There are many other, more subtle, signs of mature leadership in successful football programs. For instance, the successful program will have the right people in the right jobs. A person who is in the position most suited to him will normally do the right thing, make the right decision, and react properly, thus reducing the margin for error.

Most successful organizations seem to know why they are successful and why they win, and they expect to continue to win. Conversely, losing organizations do not know why they lose. They usually have many excuses, but rarely any answers. Unlike them, successful organizations never make excuses for losing, whether justified or not. They have the maturity to say "We didn't do our job well enough. We must improve."

Successful programs constantly seem to be making improvements. They do not waste time trying to justify errors—they concentrate on fixing problems and continuing to improve. These programs have a dedication to pursuing excellence that sustains their high quality. Such programs also seem to be characterized by excellent communication among their members. From the head coach to the student stat keepers, an open line of communication allows information to flow quickly and accurately throughout the organization.

Of course, teamwork is the most apparent element in a successful program—the feeling that everyone is working together toward the same goal. The pride that goes with being a part of a strong team effort, however small that part may be, is obvious. When the team wins, it is clear that everyone wins; when it loses, everyone shares the loss.

Finally, a sense of humor and respect for others, combined with hard work and discipline, are the sure signs of maturity and success. These ingredients must be present for success to be present—*there is no other way!*

I realize that this book contains a great deal of information. That all of the material presented here will be successfully introduced into a program during its first year is highly unlikely, and not really necessary. What cannot be properly accomplished the first year may be put on a priority list for the following year and the year after that until the task is done. Then, once a plan is implemented, you must constantly review, correct, and continue to improve or you may run the risk of regressing. Continued improvement is an important element in the "pursuit of excellence."

If you love the game of high school football as I do, you will be truly excited at having the opportunity to grow in this way, and by doing so, to contribute to the positive image of the game. The only way to do this is by demonstrating that maturity, intelligence, and leadership are as much a part of football as of any other school of learning. The desire and effort to improve, year after year, will set the dedicated head coach apart from the rest and make the sport of football a valuable asset to the school and the community.

Bibliography

Bibliography

Benhase, C.K. (1967). *Ohio High School football*. West Nyack, NY: Parker.

Brady, J.T. (1984). *Heisman: Symbol of excellence*. New York: Atheneum.

Bryant, P.W. (1968). *Building a championship football team*. Englewood Cliffs, NJ: Prentice-Hall.

Bryant, P.W., & Underwood, J. (1975). *Bear: The hard life and good times of Alabama's Coach Bryant*. New York: Bantam.

Capozzoli, T. (1981). *Complete book of football instruction*. Chicago: Contemporary Books.

Daugherty, D., & Wilson, C.B. (1970). *First and ten*. Dubuque, IA: Brown.

DeLuca, S. (1981). *The football handbook*. Middle Village, NY: Jonathan David.

Dominguez, R.H. (1979). *The complete book of sports medicine*. New York: Scribner.

Fox, E.L. (1979). *Sports physiology*. Philadelphia: Saunders.

Garfield, C.A., & Bennett, H.Z. (1985). *Peak performance*. New York: Warner.

Hammer, B. (1963). *The football coaches complete handbook*. Englewood Cliffs, NJ: Prentice-Hall.

Hayes, W.W. (1969). *Hot line to victory*. Columbus, OH: Typographic.

Hayes, W.W. (1975). *You win with people*. Columbus, OH: Typographic.

Herbert, D. (Ed.). (1981). Compiled by the American Football Coaches Association. *Football coaching*. New York: Scribner.

Holtz, H. (1984). *Beyond the résumé: How to land the job you want.* New York: McGraw-Hill.

Holtz, L. (1974). *The grass is greener.* Raleigh, NC: Litho-Graphics.

Hyman, M.D., & White, G.S. (1971). *Paterno: Football my way.* New York: MacMillan.

Iacocca, L. (1984). *Iacocca: An autobiography.* New York: Bantam.

Jefferies, S. (1985). *Coaches guide to time management study guide.* Champaign, IL: Human Kinetics.

Kozoll, C.E. (1985). *Coaches guide to time management.* Champaign, IL: Human Kinetics.

Martens, R., Christina, R.W., Harvey, J.S., & Sharkey, B.J. (1981). *Coaching young athletes.* Champaign, IL: Human Kinetics.

Mirkin, G., & Hoffman, M. (1978). *The sports medicine book.* Boston: Little Brown.

Morton, C., & Burger, R. (1984). *The courage to believe.* New York: Ballantine/Epiphany.

Parseghian, A.R., & Pagna, T. (1973). *Parseghian and Notre Dame football.* Garden City, NY: Doubleday.

Peters, S. (1962). *How to select and develop athletes for winning high school football.* Englewood Cliffs, NJ: Prentice-Hall.

Peters, T.J., & Austin, N. (1985). *A passion for excellence.* New York: Random House.

Peters, T.J., & Waterman, R.H. (1984). *In search of excellence.* New York: Warner Books.

Peterson, W.S. (1977). *The art of living treasure chest: 75 best and most inspiring essays.* New York: Simon & Schuster.

Rice, H. (1962). *How to organize football practice.* Englewood Cliffs, NJ: Prentice-Hall.

Rice, H. (1976). *Leadership in athletics: The attitude technique.* Waco, TX: Success Motivation Institute.

Royal, D. (1976). *Dance with who brung us.* Austin, TX: Jenkins Press.

Teaff, G., & Blain, S. (1975). *I believe.* Dallas: Word Books.

Thomas, L. (1959). *The vital spark.* Garden City, NY: Doubleday.

Tutko, T., & Tosi, U. (1976). *Sports psyching: Playing your best game all the time*. Los Angeles: J.P. Tarcher.

Wiebusch, J. (Ed.). (1971). *Lombardi*. Chicago, IL: Follett.

Wilkinson, C. (1973). *Sports Illustrated football*. Philadelphia: Lippincott.

Wooden, J., Sharman, W., & Seizer, B. (1975). *The Wooden-Sharman method: A guide to winning basketball*. New York: MacMillan.

Wooden, J., as told to Tobin, J. (1972). *They call me coach*. Dallas: Word Books.